624-5780

PRAYING IN THE PRESENCE OF

OUR LORD

WITH
FULTON J.
SHEEN

Praying In The Presence Of
Our Lord

WITH
FULTON J. SHEEN

MICHAEL DUBRUIEL

FR. BENEDICT J. GROESCHEL, C.F.R.
SERIES EDITOR

Our Sunday Visitor Publishing Division
Our Sunday Visitor, Inc.
Huntington, Indiana 46750

Nihil Obstat
Rev. Michael Heintz
Censor Librorum

Imprimatur
The Most Rev. John M. Darcy
Bishop of Fort Wayne-South Bend
November 9, 2001

The *Nihil Obstat* and *Imprimatur* are official declarations of ecclesiastical authority
that a book is free of doctrinal or moral error. No implication is contained therein
that those who have granted the *Nihil Obstat* and *Imprimatur* agree with the content,
opinions, or statements expressed in the work. Nor do they assume any legal
responsibility associated with publication.

Scripture quotations in this book (except for two from the *Douay-Rheims*, one from
the *New International Version*, and whatever editions were used in Bishop Sheen's
published works) are taken from two main sources: (1) the *Revised Standard Version of
the Holy Bible, Catholic Edition*, copyright ©1965, 1966 by the Division of Christian
Education of the National Council of the Churches of Christ in the United States of
America; used by permission of the copyright holder; all rights reserved; (2) the *New
American Bible* copyright © 1986, 1970 by the Confraternity of Christian Doctrine,
Inc., Washington, D.C.; used with permission, all rights reserved. Attributions are
designated by RSV (for *Revised Standard Version*) and NAB (for *New American Bible*).
The author and publisher are grateful to those publishers and others whose materials,
whether in the public domain or protected by copyright laws, have been used in one
form or another in this volume. Special thanks go to America Press, Inc., for
permission to use excerpts from Bishop Sheen's works, published by special
arrangement with the Estate of Fulton J. Sheen, c/o The Society for the Propagation
of the Faith. Every reasonable effort has been made to determine copyright holders
of excerpted materials and to secure permissions as needed. If any copyrighted
materials have been inadvertently used in this work without proper credit being
given in one form or another, please notify Our Sunday Visitor in writing so that
future printings of this work may be corrected accordingly.

ISBN: 0-87973-715-8
LCCCN: 2001135286

Cover design by Tyler Ottinger
Cover art by Robert F. McGovern
Interior design by Sherri L. Hoffman

PRINTED IN THE UNITED STATES OF AMERICA

✠

For my father, Albert Joseph Dubruiel,
who first introduced me to the great Fulton J. Sheen.
And
to the lovely Lady dressed in blue,
the Blessed Virgin Mary, Mother of the Word Incarnate,
that she may bring the reader ever closer to her Son,
Our Lord Jesus Christ.

Contents

✠

Preface by Father Andrew Apostoli, C.F.R.   9
Foreword by Father Benedict J. Groeschel, C.F.R. 13
Introduction   17
How to Use This Book   23

Part I: Sharing in the Work of Redemption   27
  1. His Work Is Finished, Ours Is Not   29
  2. Our Need for Redemption   33
  3. Members of Christ's Body   38
  4. Charity   41
  5. The Sweetest Kind of Love   45
  6. Reparation   49
  7. Contrition   53
  8. God Permits Evil for a Greater Good   57
  9. The Redemption Is Reciprocal   61
  10. The Sanctification of the Present Moment   65

**Part II: Our Lord Asks for Our
Companionship   69**
  11. Come and See   71
  12. Love Is Triune   75
  13. Tragic Words   79
  14. A Word to Sinners   82
  15. Hope   86
  16. The Divine Embrace   90

17. The Effects of the Eucharist 94
18. Mortification: Dying to Live 98
19. Meditation 101
20. Brotherhood 105

Part III: We Grow into the Likeness of Our Lord **111**
21. Christian Asceticism 113
22. Silence 117
23. Meaning in Suffering 121
24. Go-Go's — Come-Come's 125
25. The Rosary 129
26. Our Father 133
27. The New Creation 137
28. When You Fail 141
29. The Anti-Christ 145
30. Salve Regina 150

Appendix I: War and Peace **155**
31. War as a Judgment of God 156
32. The Power of God 160

Appendix II: Prayers **165**
Prayer to Obtain a Favor Through the
    Intercession of Archbishop Sheen 166
Prayer to Move the Church to Proclaim
    Archbishop Sheen a Saint 167

Sources **169**

Preface

✠

On October 2, 1979, a very moving event occurred in St. Patrick's Cathedral in New York City. Pope John Paul II, on his first papal visit to the United States, entered the cathedral with Terence Cardinal Cooke, then archbishop of New York. As the Pope and the cardinal in procession reached an open area in the sanctuary, the Holy Father paused and looked around. Then he said to Cardinal Cooke, "Where is Archbishop Sheen?"

Since there was no prearranged seating for the archbishops and bishops, the cardinal did not know. He sent his secretary to find Archbishop Sheen, who was in the crowd of prelates in the Lady Chapel behind the sanctuary area.

When Archbishop Sheen emerged into the open area where the Holy Father was waiting, a tumultuous seven-minute applause erupted from the vast crowd in the cathedral. Then the Holy Father and the archbishop embraced, and as they did so, Pope John Paul II said to Archbishop Sheen, "You have written and spoken well of the Lord Jesus. You are a loyal son of the Church!"

These memorable words of the Holy Father sum up not only the life of the late archbishop, but the abundant legacy he left behind for us to read in his books, listen to on his tapes, and watch on his videos. They will always be in demand!

And so will this fine new book, *Praying in the Presence of Our Lord with Fulton J. Sheen.* Quoting from over thirty of the archbishop's works, author Michael Dubruiel presents a choice portion of the timeless wisdom and profound insights that characterized all that Archbishop Sheen said and wrote. It is "timeless wisdom," because the archbishop himself acknowledged that it all came to him as he prayed before Jesus in the Blessed Sacrament. Since Jesus is timeless, being "the same yesterday and today and for ever" (Hebrews 13:8), the message is also timeless, being as relevant today as the day it was written. There are "profound insights" because Archbishop Sheen knew how to listen attentively to what the Spirit of God was saying to the Church (cf. Revelation 2:7). He knew how to grasp the present situation of society, and meet its challenges with the Gospel of Jesus Christ.

The author's reflections help the reader to delve more deeply into the archbishop's message, and apply it to his or her own situation. The reflections are wonderful for personal meditation and even shared with others. The brief prayer after each section brings the reflection to an inspiring conclusion.

If you are already a Bishop Sheen reader, you know the influence and appeal he can have, as the author attests in his own Introduction. If you are not, you are in for a wonderful experience!

Archbishop Sheen deeply touched and transformed many lives. I, too, can attest to this fact.

On March 16, 1967, Bishop Sheen ordained me "a priest forever" while serving as the bishop of the Diocese of Rochester, New York. Not only was he God's instrument to confer the priesthood upon me, but he was also His instrument in showing me by his words and example how to be a priest close to the Heart of Jesus. At the end of the homily he gave at my Ordination Mass, the archbishop said, "The joy of being a priest will grow!" How prophetic he has been!

In turn, I believe that through his message in this treasure of a book by Michael Dubruiel, the Christian joy of anyone who reads it will likewise grow.

FATHER ANDREW APOSTOLI, C.F.R.
December 9, 2001
Twenty-second Anniversary of
Archbishop Sheen's Death

Foreword

✠

---

*I*t is a great pleasure to add this new volume to our collection of books inviting people to pray in the presence of the Holy Eucharist. This book recalls the powerful teaching and witness of Archbishop Fulton J. Sheen, one of my own boyhood heroes. Michael Dubruiel has done an outstanding job of reviewing the immense body of sermons and writings of Archbishop Sheen and composing a prayerful anthology of his work. He has added to this a fine set of meditations, which obviously are drawn from many years of study of the works of Archbishop Sheen.

Those of us who go back to the golden days of radio and even of early television remember the amazing popularity of Archbishop Sheen. In an America that retained some of the old-style anti-Catholic prejudice, he was welcomed by immense radio audiences as a spokesman for Christianity. He was popular with Catholic and non-Catholic Christians and, in fact, with members of other religious faiths. Never once did Bishop Sheen back away from a witness to the Catholic faith, although he had a very wide interfaith audience. He was obviously a man of prayer, deep meditation, and profound belief. This book will bring into the Eucharistic meditations and life of anyone who uses it faithfully an intelligent and deeply spiritual expression of the truths that Our Lord Jesus Christ left to His Church and the teachings that have developed as a result of His revelation.

Since Michael Dubruiel has given ample instructions on how to pray with the writings of Archbishop Sheen, instructions that can be useful for any kind of theological meditation, it is not necessary to do what I have done in previous volumes in this series. If you are not familiar with meditating on great theological truths, this volume will open up new experiences for you. People who have had a deficient religious education in the confusing decades at the end of the twentieth century will find this book a gold mine of theological truths that they believe but that they do not adequately understand. This is not only a meditation book, it is also a catechism for people who have been inadequately trained in the content of their faith.

Father Andrew Apostoli, my fellow member of the Franciscan Friars of the Renewal, has added his own touching words to this book. His own remarkable experience of having been ordained a priest by Archbishop Sheen is something that will warm the hearts of everyone who uses this volume. Father Andrew reminds us of the greeting of our Holy Father when he embraced Archbishop Sheen at St. Patrick's Cathedral. I was there in the sanctuary at that very moment tending to the non-Catholic representatives who had come to greet the Pope and I recall very well the tumultuous greeting that Archbishop Sheen received as he embraced the Pope.

I also knew the quiet and humble man that Archbishop Sheen became at the end of his life. The Carmelite Sisters for the Aged and Infirm were preparing to receive him at the Mary Manning Walsh Home shortly before his death. They have told me how impressed they were by the humility and gentleness of this man who had received an immense amount of applause in his life. The Holy Spirit, who had guided him in his preaching, was now preparing him for his final appearance by giving him a very humble and gentle way as he prepared to leave this world.

Along with the editors of Our Sunday Visitor, I am very honored to have the opportunity to participate in this recognition of one of the great apostles of the Catholic Church in the United States.

FATHER BENEDICT J. GROESCHEL, C.F.R.

Introduction

⊹

I still remember walking into the living room of our family's home in Winchester, New Hampshire, and seeing my father transfixed in front of the television set watching a bishop preach. My father, not easily impressed, clearly was, by this man's preaching. The year was 1975. A local station out of Massachusetts was broadcasting reruns of the famous "Life Is Worth Living" series of Bishop Sheen's that had originally aired from 1951 to1957, first on the DuMont Network, and later on ABC to a national audience. At the time I do not remember personally being that taken by the bishop; but the fact that my father was, left its impression on me.

My introduction to Archbishop Sheen came about in the last year of his life. At that time I was serving in the United States Army and had just been sent to serve a one-year tour of duty in Turkey at a small military outpost there. Upon my arrival I went to the Chaplain's Office and inquired if he might have any Catholic reading material. He replied that he did not but that the previous chaplain who happened to have been a Catholic priest had left behind a set of tapes. I was free to have them if I wanted them.

The tapes were recordings of a retreat that Archbishop Sheen had given to priests.

Bored at the time, I figured that I would give them a hearing. I could never have imagined the effect they would have on me. From the very first talk I found myself won over. Here was a Catholic who knew the Scriptures and preached with authority. Here was a man of God!

I listened to the tapes over and over, amazed that no matter how many times I played them how new the material seemed to me. From that day forward I sought out every book and tape by Bishop Sheen that I could get my hands on, devouring them in my spare moments in that faraway land.

I made a vow that upon my return to the United States in December of 1979 I would search out Bishop Sheen. Ironically, upon my assignment to a military base in Virginia, the first night there I was shocked to hear on the news that Fulton Sheen had died. I would never get the chance to meet him in person, on this earth anyway. But I felt that he was now more present to me than he ever could have been while still alive.

Even though no one had declared him a saint, I often sought his intercession and found that this often met with favorable results. I had no doubt that Fulton Sheen was someone who had used his God-given gifts to the greater honor and glory of God. Truly he was a modern-day golden-tongued preacher like St. John Chrysostom.

I, of course, was not alone in my appreciation of Archbishop Sheen. Millions were touched by him from the time of his birth in 1895 until his death in December 1979, and many more are discovering him anew now some twenty years after his death. His "Life Is Worth Living" series (both the original black-and-white show of the 1950s and a later version that the archbishop made in color) is once again broadcast nationally, this time on the Eternal Word Network (EWTN). His books are being reprinted at an astonishing pace. Books like the one you hold in your hand compile his writings on certain subjects.

And there is talk of sainthood. In December of 1999, on the twentieth anniversary of his death, Cardinal John O'Connor authorized the private investigation into the life of Archbishop Sheen by the Archbishop Fulton John Sheen Foundation.

A bishop recently told me that he was privileged to meet Bishop Sheen when he was a young priest. He said that Bishop Sheen had taken him aside and given him a very personal message about the future. What Bishop Sheen had told the young priest had come to pass in his life. He now says that he has no doubt that Sheen was a mystic.

When you read the passages he wrote years ago included in this book, you too will reach that conclusion. I have been amazed as I chose various texts from his writings, some written over sixty-five years ago, to discover how relevant they are to the present.

Bishop Sheen used the gifts that God had given him and perhaps developed some that were not natural to him. One of his biographers tells us that when he was in the seminary, the coach of the debate team told him that he was a horrible speaker. If that were true at the time, then it is truly amazing that the greatest Catholic preacher of the twentieth century was someone not defeated by this early judgment. Bishop Sheen worked tirelessly to improve his preaching ability because the message that he had to deliver was of the utmost urgency! Would that many modern-day homilists follow his example.

The decision to include Archbishop Sheen in the *Praying in the Presence of Our Lord* series was essentially made as soon as the series was conceived. There is no one in the modern Church who has done more to popularize the practice of praying in the presence of Our Lord in the Blessed Sacrament. No matter to whom Archbishop Sheen was speaking (including non-Catholics, and even non-Christians), he never tired of recommending the practice of making a daily holy hour in front of the Blessed Sacrament.

This was not advice that Bishop Sheen gave without practicing it himself. Indeed he never missed a day for over sixty years, from the day of his priestly ordination until his death on the chapel floor in Our Lord's presence. There were times that he was so tired that he slept through the hour (he mentions one such time in his autobiography), but nonetheless he was there.

Bishop Sheen credited his practice of the holy hour as the fuel that fired his preaching, missionary work, and apostolic activities. Thomas C. Reeves recounts the text of a talk that Bishop Sheen gave a few years before his death in his excellent biography of the archbishop entitled *America's Bishop: The Life and Times of Fulton J. Sheen* (Encounter Books, San Francisco, 2001). The event was the formal dedication of the Archbishop Fulton John Sheen Archives in Rochester, New York, and the bishop said that all of his written works could not explain him, then he told a story:

> "Very often, when I go to Paris . . . I visit Carmes. It was an old Carmelite monastery, but after the French Revolution was converted into one of the dormitory buildings of the *Institut Catholique*, and there is one room that I always visit. It's at the end of a corridor . . . and over the desk was carved a peephole. It was the room of the great preacher Lacordaire, and as he sat at that desk he could look through that peephole, and what did he see? He looked on the tabernacle — he looked on the Blessed Sacrament. It was that that made Lacordaire great."
>
> There is no complete explanation of Fulton J. Sheen in these books, in these tapes. You have to look for a secret from the outside, where knowledge is converted into wisdom, and that is done only at the feet of Christ and his Blessed Sacrament. So may all who enter this room be reminded of a peephole. Look through it, and you'll explain Fulton John Sheen.
>
> — From *America's Bishop:*
> *The Life and Times of Fulton J. Sheen*

It is fitting that this work continue Bishop Sheen's influence on leading others to meet Our Lord in His sacred Eucharistic Presence and bringing them to a deeper appreciation of the great gift that Our Lord has given us through his enduring presence.

MICHAEL DUBRUIEL
Feast of St. Thérèse of the Child Jesus
October 1, 2001

How to Use This Book

✣

This book is arranged into three main sections, each of them dealing with three immense blessings that Bishop Sheen believed we would receive if we practice regularly praying in the presence of Our Lord. These blessings include:

- *Sharing in Our Lord's work of redemption.*
- *Fulfilling Our Lord's desire for our companionship.*
- *Growing into the likeness of Our Lord.*

Each of these sections contains ten meditations drawn from Bishop Sheen's works. Along with the bishop's words, the following are included: Scripture, a reflection, points to ponder, and a closing prayer.

There are two appendixes in the book.

The first is dedicated to Bishop Sheen's thoughts on war and the power of God that presents material in a similar style as the rest of the book. This section was added after September 11, 2001, when foreign terrorists hijacked four American commercial airliners, ramming two of them into the World Trade Center towers in New York, another into the Pentagon, and crashing a fourth in Pennsylvania when some of the passengers evidently fought with the hijackers. Bishop Sheen penned the material in this appendix over sixty years ago; but like the other material in the book written by him, it is as relevant today as it was then and to whatever the future might hold.

The second appendix contains two prayers. One is a prayer to be used in order to obtain a favor through the archbishop's intercession, while the other is for his canonization. This appendix also includes contact information to report any favors received or any material the reader might have to offer in the investigation into Bishop Sheen's life.

Readers should use whatever parts of the meditations are helpful to them during any particular prayer period. Following the ancient practice of *Lectio Divina* ("divine reading"), readers should stop whenever some word or passage strikes them and dwell upon it for awhile. Readers are encouraged to ask the Lord what it is that He wants to reveal to them in these words.

Readers may find that they are able to use the same meditation over and over. Whatever the Lord wishes should be their desire.

The reflections and questions are my invention and should not be confused as that of Bishop Sheen's. I have attempted to draw upon his thought in these sections, but clearly the focus of the book is the great writing that is his own.

I have tried for the most part to present material in this book that is drawn from books of Bishop Sheen's that are currently out of print. The archbishop wrote so many books during his lifetime on

such a wide variety of subjects that what is presented here is merely a taste. I hope for you, the
reader, a good taste, one that will leave you hungry
for the Bread of Life.

I.

Sharing in the Work of Redemption

What? Could you not watch one hour with me?
— MATTHEW 26:40 *(Douay-Rheims)*

Jesus spoke these words to His disciples in the Garden of Gethsemane, yet as I read them I hear them with the voice of Archbishop Sheen, who was able to bring passages such as this alive with his unique style. Also carried with his intonation is the meaning that he gave to them, that the words that Jesus spoke to His disciples some two thousand years ago in that garden on the Mount of Olives echo throughout history and are spoken again and again to each disciple — in other words, to you and to me.

The Lord asks us to watch with Him, to share in His work, which although complete on Calvary long ago is ongoing in that the tree of the cross continually bears new fruit in us, His disciples. The work of redemption then continues and will not be complete until all of us are brought to the foot of the cross and believe that Our Lord has the power to save us.

Our Lord speaks to us as we come into His presence and asks us to join Him.

In this section we reflect with Archbishop Sheen on how Our Lord wishes us to share in His work, which is the work of redemption.

I
His Work Is Finished, Ours Is Not

When Jesus had taken the wine, he said, "It is finished."
And bowing his head, he handed over the spirit.
— JOHN 19:30 (NAB)

✠

Bishop Sheen

Our Blessed Lord's work is finished. But is *ours?* When
He said, *"it* is finished," He did not mean that the
opportunities of His life had ended; He meant that
His work was done so perfectly that nothing could
be added to it to make it more perfect — but with us,
how seldom that is true. Too many of us *end* our lives,
but few of us see them *finished*. A sinful life may end,
but a sinful life is never a finished life.

If our lives just "end," our friends will ask: "How
much did he leave?" But if our life is "finished," our
friends will ask: "How much did he take with him?"
A finished life is not measured by years but by deeds;
not by the time spent in the vineyard, but by the
work done. In a short time a man may fulfill many
years; even those who come at the eleventh hour may
finish their lives; even those who come to God like
the thief at the last breath, may finish their lives in the
Kingdom of God. Not for them the sad word of re-
gret: "Too late, O ancient Beauty, have I loved Thee."

Our Lord finished His work, but we have not finished ours. He pointed the way we must follow. He laid down the Cross at the finish, but we must take it up. He finished Redemption in His physical Body, but we have not finished it in His Mystical Body. He has finished salvation, we have not yet applied it to our souls. He has finished the Temple, but we must live in it. He has finished the model Cross, we must fashion ours to its pattern. He has finished sowing the seed, we must reap the harvest. He has finished filling the chalice, but we have not finished drinking its refreshing draughts. He has planted the wheat field; we must gather it into our barns. He has finished the Sacrifice of Calvary; we must finish the Mass.

The Crucifixion was not meant to be an inspirational drama, but a pattern act on which to model our lives. We are not meant to sit and watch the Cross as something done and ended like the life of Socrates. *What was done on Calvary avails for us only in the degree that we repeat it in our own lives.*

— From *Calvary and the Mass*

Reflection

Bishop Sheen often quoted St. Paul's boast that what Paul preached was Christ and Him Crucified. Bishop Sheen imitated St. Paul in his preaching and in his writing. Here in this passage taken from *Calvary and the Mass* we see again the centrality of the cross of Jesus for the bishop.

Jesus spoke from the cross that His mission was finished and so it is, but Bishop Sheen invites us to not think of our lives as finished just yet.

It is an ancient spiritual practice to meditate on one's eventual death not out of a macabre sense but in order to better understand our lives. We project ourselves into the future and examine how we are living our lives toward that end.

The inventor of dynamite was privileged in his life to read his obituary one morning after a mistaken report circulated that he had died the night before. It turned out that if he had indeed died on that night he would have been remembered as the founder of a destructive element that led to the ruin of countless lives.

This was not the way that the inventor wished to be remembered, so for the rest of his life his aim was turned to making a positive contribution to humanity. The faulty obituary was a moment of grace for him. We now remember Alfred Nobel each year as recipients of the Nobel Peace Prize are announced.

It is not too late for you. What does the Lord want you to do?

+ + +

Spend some time reflecting on the following:

1. Imagine that through some mistake while you are alive the report goes out that you have died. How would your life be summed up in your obituary in tomorrow's paper? (You may find it helpful to write out your own obituary.) Ask God for the grace to know what you need to change in your life.

2. Imagine that you are an observer at your own funeral. Who attends? Is there someone whose absence bothers you? Is there anyone that you are surprised to see there? What are people talking about as they reflect on your life? Again ask God for the grace to know what you should learn from this exercise.

3. Imagine that you are standing at the judgment seat of God. Imagine God loving you and welcoming you into His presence. How does this make you feel? What does God's love reveal to you about your life? Is there a task that God asks you if you have completed? Ask God for the grace to take up the unfinished business of your life.

Prayer

Lord, open my eyes to see what it is that you want me to do. Give me the grace necessary to focus on what it is that I am to do in my life. Help me always to seek your will in all that I do. Amen.

2
Our Need for Redemption

"Rejoice with me, for I have found my sheep which was lost."
— LUKE 15:6 (RSV)

+

Bishop Sheen

First, man is not an angel, nor is he a devil. He is not intrinsically corrupt (as theologians began claiming four hundred years ago) nor is he intrinsically divine (as philosophers began saying fifty years ago). Rather, man has aspirations to good which he finds it impossible to realize completely by himself; at the same time, he has an inclination toward evil which solicits him away from these ideals. He is like a man who is down in a well through his own stupidity. He knows he ought not to be there, but cannot get out by himself. Or, to change the picture, he is like a clock whose mainspring is broken. He needs to be fixed on the inside, but the repairs must be supplied from without. He is mistaken if he is an optimist, who believes evolution to be the mainspring, or a pessimist who believes that nobody can fix him. He is a creature who can run well again, but only if some watchmaker will have the kindness to repair him.

Second, this conflict has all the appearances of being due to the abuse of human freedom. As the drunkard is what he is, because of an act of choice, so human nature seems to have lost the original goodness with which a Good God endowed it, through an act of choice. As St. Augustine said, "Whatever we are, we are not what we ought to be." The origin of this conflict has been told by medieval and modern theologians through the analogy of music. Picture an orchestra on stage with a celebrated conductor directing the beautiful symphony he himself composed. Each member of the orchestra is free to follow the conductor and thus to produce harmony. But each member is also free to disobey the conductor. Suppose one of the musicians deliberately plays a false note and then induces a violinist alongside of him to do the same. Having heard the discord, the conductor can do one of two things. He could either strike his baton and order the measure replayed, or he could ignore the discord. It would make no difference which he did, for that discord has already gone out into space at a certain temperature at the rate of about 1100 feet a second. On and on it goes, affecting even the infinitesimally small radiations of the universe. As the stone dropped in a pond causes a ripple which affects the most distant shore, so this discord affects even the stars. As long as time endures, somewhere in God's Universe there is disharmony, introduced by the free will of man.

Could that discord be stopped? Not by man himself, for man could never reach it; time is irreversible, and man is localized in space. It *could*, however, be stopped by the Eternal coming out of His agelessness into time, laying hold of the false note, arresting it in its flight. But would it still be discord in God's Hands? No! Not if God wrote a *new* symphony and made the false note its first note! Then all would be harmony again.

— From *Peace of Soul*

Reflection

There are two parts to this passage of Bishop Sheen's that capture the eye. First, man has aspirations that he cannot achieve without help from some outside power; second, man is tempted away from these ideals by an inclination to evil. Both point to the need for a savior.

Within each of us there is a longing for something more. What that "more" is can be greatly confused in our lives. Some may think that their happiness lies in having more wealth, others better health, and still others long for some living creature that will somehow complete them. However, the great spiritual writers, many of whom made the journey down all the false roads of longing before finding the true road to peace, have pointed out that what our hearts truly long for is God.

In the presence of the Lord what do we pray for? Wisdom to know and trust that if we have what we need for our sustenance we are truly blessed? Knowledge to discern what paths we should take that will lead us to eternal salvation? Or do we pray for something that secretly we really believe will make us happy but is not God?

Many of our false longings reflect both the sins that we have committed in the past and the sins that have been committed against us in the past. We hope to redeem ourselves either in our own eyes or the eyes of our wealthy, healthy, satiated neighbors. But the lesson of countless experiences has taught us that none of the "false redeemers" can save us. No matter how much money we acquire, it is never enough. Our health may be great, but we still continue to age and none too gracefully. Every attempt to be satiated quickly leaves us hungering again.

Only in God. God alone.

+ + +

Spend some time reflecting on the following:

1. What are your aspirations in life? What keeps you from fulfilling them? Do you see them as God-inspired or are they from another source? Ask God for the grace to discern His will for you.

2. Look to Jesus as your redeemer. What does Jesus save you from? What have you not allowed Jesus to redeem you from? Ask God for the grace to be open to His free gifts.

3. Spend some time meditating on the Beatitudes in Matthew 5:3-12. Reflect on the meaning of true happiness. Ask God for the grace to direct you toward that which will bring you true contentment in your life.

Prayer

Lord, reveal to me what I ought to be and then give me the grace to be that person. Redeem me from all the hurts that I have inflicted upon myself and allowed others to inflict upon me. Amen.

3
Members of Christ's Body

If [one] part suffers, all the parts suffer with it;
if one part is honored, all the parts share its joy.
— 1 Corinthians 12:26 (NAB)

✠

Bishop Sheen

In medicine, when a patient is suffering from anemia, blood will be transferred from a healthy person to cure the sick of that condition. Skin is grafted from the back to the face to repair a burn. If blood can be transfused and skin grafted, then prayers and sacrifices can be transmitted to the sick members of the Mystical Body of Christ. The motivation for a Holy Hour is reparation. We pray for those who do not pray, we make acts of faith in the Real Presence for those who lack or who have lost the faith. In a word, we are their victims, like Christ, innocent but one with their guilt in the progressive redemption of mankind.

— From *Those Mysterious Priests*

Reflection

There is perhaps no greater way to share in the redemptive work of Christ than by praying for others. Using the image of the physical body, Bishop Sheen reminds us of how one part of the body can help another part, so too he says in the Mystical Body of Christ. Our prayer can have a positive effect on others, often in ways that we may never know.

Most people know that Dorothy Day was a pacifist, but I doubt many know why. Her beliefs were based on the *Baltimore Catechism*, which had taught her that every baptized person was a temple of the Holy Spirit. She reasoned that if that were so, then she could never support the physical attack of places where human beings who were both actual and potential temples of the Holy Spirit resided.

But Dorothy's pacifism was not passive. In fact, she once stated, "If we are not going to use our spiritual weapons, let us by all means arm and prepare." She believed in the power of God's ability to do what was humanly impossible, namely to bring about peace.

Do we divide the world into friend or foe? Or do we see all people as actual and potential members of the Body of Christ?

We share in Our Lord's redemptive work when we use the spiritual weapons that He has put at our disposal to combat the real enemy of all — the devil. In the same way that we might donate blood to help someone in desperate need of a transfusion, let us donate our prayers to those in most need of the Blood of Christ.

+ + +

Spend some time reflecting on the following:

1. Ask God to make you aware of who needs to be prayed for today. Remember both the living and

the dead. Call to mind the person as you ask God to bless that particular individual.

2. Reflect on whose prayers may be responsible for your own faith. Spend some time giving thanks to God for the people of faith who have passed on the faith to you. Ask God for the grace to imitate them.

3. Meditating on the image that Bishop Sheen presents in his story of someone needing a skin graft or blood transfusion, imagine that certain parts of the Mystical Body, the Church, might be in need of similar aid. What images present themselves to you? Ask God for the grace of healing to come upon the Church wherever it is needed.

Prayer

Lord, give me a living sense of the Church as your Mystical Body. Help me to feel the pain and the needs of others so that I may respond to them as I would my own. Amen.

4
Charity

"Truly, I say to you, as you did it to one of the least of these my brethren, you did it to me."
— MATTHEW 25:40 (RSV)

✠

Bishop Sheen

Charity, in brief, centers about two realities — human natures, who dispense or receive benefices; and things, like gold and silver, clothing and food. Charity embraces in its scope both what we are and what we have.

Since charity involves these two great visibilities of the world, flesh and things, it is fitting that both of them should have figured in the supreme act of charity, which was the Redemption of mankind. And actually both of them did hold a prominent place. First, Christ assumed a human nature and that was the Incarnation; second, He spiritualized material things — and these were the sacraments.

But the Incarnate did not exhaust Himself in the Incarnation. The Incarnational process continues. Charity workers are therefore to do with these great realities what He did. First of all, we are to offer our individual human natures to Him, that He may continue the work of His Incarnation — human natures with which He might visit the sick, instruct the ignorant, counsel the doubtful, open blind eyes to the light of His sunlight, unstop deaf ears to the music of the human voice. Second, we are to make use of things, our possessions, our talents, as kinds of sacraments, each one of which has pronounced over it the consecrating words: *"This* is offered on account of you, O Lord!" in order that the whole universe may become sacramentalized for His honor and glory.

This is the philosophy of Catholic charity, and since the day charity became organic with us, it has never been quite right to say that God is in His Heaven and all's right with the world; for Christ has left the heavens to set it right, and is found amongst us, even as we talk.

— From *Old Errors and New Labels*

Reflection

Bishop Sheen spent sixteen years of his life raising money for the missions as the director of the Society for the Propagation of the Faith. His devotion to the Lord in the Blessed Sacrament and his strong belief led him to find the Lord in the least of his brethren.

We may gaze on the bread now become the Sacred Body of Our Lord with great faith, but hopefully that same devotion leads us to encounter that same Lord in the hungry, the thirsty, the stranger, the imprisoned when we leave the chapel and go out into the world.

Bishop Sheen often spoke of the continuing Incarnation of Our Lord in His Mystical Body, the

Church. Just as God humbled Himself to become human, He calls each of us to continue this action — to be His presence in the world — in our own lives. We are to be Jesus to one another.

We, like the Sacred Bread that we receive at Mass, are to be changed into the likeness of Him who becomes our food. Our actions in the world should reflect the actions of Jesus. With everything we do in our daily lives we should ask ourselves, "Is this what Our Lord would do in this situation?"

But this conversion goes further, as the bishop says in this beautiful meditation. We are to change the material things that we have in this world too, converting them from their banal use so that they become the very building blocks of the Kingdom of God.

Our encounter with God should be like that of Cornelius in the Acts of the Apostles who, when converted to Christ, was joined by his entire household who converted with him. For us this means that everything we are and everything we own is called to share in our conversion to Christ.

✝ ✝ ✝

Spend some time reflecting on the following:

1. How much do I allow myself to have the mind of Christ? Am I open to Christ operating through my human nature or do I allow false humility and pride to hold me back from being truly Christlike? Ask God to give you the grace to show you what you need to let go of in your life in order to be more like Him.

2. How do I use the material possessions I have acquired in my life? Am I like the foolish rich man who planned on building bigger barns for his acquired good fortune, not realizing that his life was at an end and others would inherit his wealth? Ask God for the grace to be a good steward of His gifts.

3. Spend some time thanking God for the many blessings you have received from Him in your life. Ask the Holy Spirit to give you the grace to be thankful at all times and for every good thing that God blesses you with in your life.

Prayer

Take, O Lord, all my liberty. Receive my memory, my understanding, and my will. You have given me all that I am and all that I possess. I return it all to you and surrender it to the guidance of your will. Give me only your love and your grace. With these I am rich enough and ask for nothing more.

— St. Ignatius of Loyola

5
The Sweetest Kind of Love

*"These things have I spoken to you, that my joy may
be in you, and that your joy may be full."*
— JOHN 15:11 (RSV)

Bishop Sheen

Hence, whenever and wherever there is an intense
and passionate love of Christ and Him Crucified, sacrifice involved in crushing anything which keeps one
away from Him is not felt pain but the sweetest kind
of love, for what is pain but sacrifice without love.
The saint does not view sacrifice as an executioner
with a sword who will take away his life, but as a yoke
that is sweet and a burden that is light. The devout do
not hate life because life hates them or because they
have drunk of its dregs and found them bitter, but
because they love God more and in loving God more
they dislike anything which would tear Him away.
Oh, could the world but realize that the love of Christ
Crucified so possesses thousands and tens of thousands of souls that they would rather lose all the world
and the riches thereof than one second of intimacy
with Him at the foot of the cross. Could it but sense
the passionless passion and wild tranquility with which
such souls each morning rush to the Communion
rail to enjoy intimate union with their changeless and

understanding Friend, Jesus in the Eucharist. Could it but dimly guess how these Christ-loving hearts rejoice in carrying a cross in order that by sharing in His death they might also share in His resurrection! Sacrifice for them is not a loss, but an exchange; not a suffering, but a dedication; not a foregoing of the enjoyable, but a conversion of passing pleasures into an eternal and unchangeable joy. Sacrifice for them is not pain, but love. Their only pain, in fact, is their inability to do more for their Beloved.

— From *The Moral Universe*

Reflection

The greatest temptation that each of us faces in life is that which appears to be good but in fact revelation has revealed as evil. This was the dilemma of Eve in the Garden of Eden and it has not changed for any of us since. What God asks often seems to be difficult and not in our best interest; yet, as Bishop Sheen points out, with the light of the cross and the knowledge of the immense love that God has for us we see things more clearly.

God's love is the impetus for us to choose wisely. If we are secure that God loves us, then we will seek to do His will in all things. We will believe that what God has revealed is true and that it is in our best interest to follow it. We will act with knowledge that God's love will empower us to do what is right.

There are many things that are sinful that appear good on the surface. People fall in love, and sexual expression can seem "good"; but God has revealed through the Scriptures and the Church that sex outside of marriage is sinful. Hoarding money may seem like the right thing to do, saving for a rainy day, but God has revealed that greed is sinful. And the list can go on and on. As in the case of Eve the "fruit looks good," but God has revealed that it is deadly. What choice will we make?

In the choices we make daily we either contribute toward the salvation of the world or work against it. We either share in Our Lord's journey to the cross or we take an easier route. But as Bishop Sheen says, if we really believe that God loves us, the cross is not a horrible symbol of torture but a sweet reward.

+ + +

Spend some time reflecting on the following:

1. What choices are you facing in your life right now? What do you feel God wishes for you to do in regard to these choices? Ask God for the grace to do His will in all things.

2. Place your entire life before the presence of God. Is there any area that you feel uncomfortable revealing to God? Is there any area of your life that you are ignoring for fear or knowledge that God would not be pleased with the choices you are making here? Ask God for the grace to trust in His mercy and to confess any sins that may still be negatively influencing your life.

3. Spend some time gazing at a crucifix. See in Our Crucified Lord the love that God has for you. Ask God to help you accept His love in your life.

Prayer

*Lord, send your Holy Spirit into our lives so
that we may see with your eyes what is the best
path to take in our daily lives. Give us the grace we
need to always choose wisely and to be empowered
by your love in all of our actions. Amen.*

6
Reparation

"If my people who are called by my name humble themselves, and pray and seek my face, and turn from their wicked ways, then I will hear from heaven, and will forgive their sin and heal their land."
— CHRONICLES 7:14 (RSV)

✠

Bishop Sheen

Our modern world very seldom thinks of the relationship of a world crisis to guilt. The modern world practically ignores guilt as responsibility for the violation of a moral law. A man who disobeys one of God's physical laws, for example, that he should eat to live, after four or five days suffers a headache. It is just as vain to deny that the breaking of moral laws has consequences as to deny that the breaking of physical laws produces certain effects. Unfortunately, many live amidst crises, trials, cold wars, and political disorders without any sense of guilt. They fail to see a connection between what is happening in the world order and the way we live, think, and move. This denial of responsibility reminds us of a husband and wife who went to the doctor. The doctor asked the husband, "What is wrong with you, sir?"

He said, *"I* eat too many cherries."

The wife said, "At the bottom of cocktail glasses."

As he blamed the sickness on cherries and not on alcohol, so too many in our modern world forget that perhaps our world headache may be due to the way we have conducted ourselves before our fellow man and before God, rather than to our political cherries. . . .

Nations, too, can get in the habit of denying that their trials, the hatred of other nations, their insecurity, and the threat of Communism may be related to their moral failings. It is too superficial a justification for any nation to blame another for its crises.

Granted now that nations as well as individuals can violate God's laws, it follows that the evil that brings us to the tragic predicament must be expiated. Greek drama and all the great philosophies of the East and West are full of the idea that guilt must be atoned for. There is no British God, no American God. God is the Father of all men, and His Lordship is exercised over all history. God's Will and man's will are interlocked in every heart and in every nation. When man's will rebels against God's Will, man creates a tragic situation, which in the person is a sense of guilt, and in the community of nations, a crisis. Our tragedy today is due basically to the human will opposing the Divine Will.

— From *Life Is Worth Living*

Reflection

There are two ways to look at the statement "War is God's punishment for man's sins." One is to put the focus on God causing the war to punish the innocent as well as the guilty. The other way to look at it is that our breaking of God's laws — that is, our sins — causes bad things like war to happen. We reap what we sow.

When we watch the news at night and see the horrible acts committed around the world, do we walk away from it thinking about our responsibility for what we have just seen?

Do we see any connection between the devaluing of human life in our nation and our nation's acceptance of legalized abortion?

Do we see any connection between the way we treat our neighbors and the way our children treat one another?

Putting something else first over God is what sin is all about, and like a cancer that grows and devours an organism, sin not only destroys our relationship with God but our relationship with our fellow humans and indeed even with creation itself.

God is more powerful than any sin though. This time in His presence is a chance for a new beginning. When Jesus prayed in the Garden of Gethsemane, an angel was sent to strengthen Him for what lay ahead. If the Son of God needed an angel to strengthen Him to carry out the will of the Father, how much more so do we?

Many of us stop by focusing on our own limitations. We have tried and tried to be better but have failed and failed again. But look to Jesus. His prayer is honest and He realizes that He needs help . . . most of us never get to this point in our lives. We need help to carry out the will of God.

+ + +

Spend some time reflecting on the following:

1. Reflect on the state of the world. What actions of yours have contributed to the lack of love in the world? Ask the Holy Spirit to enlighten you and give you knowledge of your sins. Pray for the grace to be sorry for them and to experience true contrition.

2. Reflect on the sin of Adam and Eve. Imagine that daily you face the same decision as they did by how you reverence God and how you treat your neighbors as well as yourself. Ask for the grace to feel horror when confronted with sin in your life.

3. Meditate on Jesus' prayer in the Garden of Gethsemane. How can you imitate Jesus in His prayer to the Father? Ask God for the grace to trust in Him no matter how dark the hour.

Prayer

*Lord, help me to see how every sinful choice
that I make contributes to the chaos and crisis
that exist in the world. May this time that I spend
in your presence lessen the evil in the world
and change the way that I live in it. Amen.*

7
Contrition

"Daughters of Jerusalem, do not weep for me,
but weep for yourselves and for your children."
— LUKE 23:28 (RSV)

✠

Bishop Sheen

Of all things on earth, that which we know least is ourselves. We know the sins and the defects of others a thousand times better than we know our own; and we see immediately the mote in our neighbor's eye, but not the beam in our own eyes. That great truth was illuminated on the way to Calvary. The pious women of Jerusalem, though quite unafraid to show their piety before impious men, saw only the suffering Jesus whom they loved; they did not see the loving Christ who suffered *for them*. They sympathized with His pain, but they did not see themselves as the cause of that pain. It was *their* sins — and ours as well — which He took upon Himself. And as if to bring that truth home to us all, there welled up from the depths of His sacred heart these words: "Weep not for me, but weep for yourselves."

O Jesus, let me see the connection between my sins and your Calvary. Let me not weep for you apart from me, but for you on account of me. Let me see that if I had been less proud, the crown of thorns would have been less piercing; that if I had been less selfish, the cross would have been less heavy; that if I had been less sinful, the road to Calvary would have been shorter. Give me the grace to weep for my sins. And may my fountain of tears become, through the example of your love, a fountain of everlasting joy.

— From *The Way of the Cross*

Reflection

Our Lord died for our sins. Every time we reject God in choosing to do evil we stand in the courtyard of Pilate and yell with the crowd, "Crucify Him! Crucify Him!"

Our Lord in return looks upon us with love. He looks on us with the same love that a parent has for a wayward child, but He goes a step further because He sees the damage and destruction we are choosing in our sinful acts and is willing to take that damage and destruction upon Himself in order to save us.

There are two ways to look at a crucifix. One is to see the great love that God has for us. He sees the ruin that we were making of our lives but was willing to lower Himself to take on our human flesh and to die a horrible death in order to save us. Another way to look at the cross is to notice the pain and suffering that is the result of choosing anything other than God, to see in the scourges, the nail wounds, the crown of thorns, and the pierced side of Our Lord the autobiography of our sinful choices.

The lesson is the same — God loves us.

Bishop Sheen was not afraid to preach the hard sayings of the Gospel and to drive home the point that to choose anything besides God is foolishness. Some might even refer to the bishop's style of preaching as "hellfire and brimstone." But one should never forget that the real message of the bishop's preaching was always highlighted by the way he ended every sermon: "God love you."

In the presence of the Lord, reacquaint yourself with Him and see in His will for you a plan that will lead you to a more fruitful life.

+ + +

Spend some time reflecting on the following:

1. Using a crucifix, meditate on the Lord's passion and His deep and abiding love for you. If you had been at the foot of the cross, what words might Jesus have spoken to you?

2. Using a crucifix, meditate on the wounds of the Lord and how they are caused by your sins. Reflect on how you might ease the pain of the crucified Lord by your future choices.

3. Meditate on how God's love is greater than a parent's love for their children. If you have a child, reflect on how much you love that child and how much more God loves each of us, His children. Ask God for the grace to be assured of His love for you.

Prayer

O Jesus, help me to understand the destructiveness of my sins by always keeping your cross before my eyes. May I ever be strengthened by your love to do what is holy and God's will. Amen.

8
God Permits Evil for a Greater Good

But Joseph said to them, "Fear not, for am I in the place of God? As for you, you meant evil against me; but God meant it for good, to bring it about that many people should be kept alive, as they are today."
— GENESIS 50:19-20 (RSV)

Bishop Sheen

God permits evil things for the reason of a greater good related to His love and the salvation of our souls.

God does permit evil. In the strong language of Scripture: "He that spared not even his own Son; but delivered Him up for us all" (Romans 8:32). Our Lord told Judas: "This is your hour" (Luke 22:53). Evil does have its hour. All that it can do within that hour is put out the lights of the world. But God has His day.

The evil of the world is inseparable from human freedom, and hence the cost of destroying the world's evil would be the destruction of human freedom. Certainly none of us want to pay that high a price, particularly since God would never permit evil unless He could draw some good from it.

God can draw good out of evil because, while the power of doing evil is ours, the effects of our evil deeds are outside our control, and, therefore, in the hands of

God. You are free to break the law of gravitation, but you have no control over the effects of throwing yourself off of the Washington Monument.

The brethren of Joseph were free to toss him into a well, but from that point on Joseph was in God's hands. Rightly did he say to his brethren: "You intended it for evil, but God for good." The executioners were free to nail Our Lord to the cross, Judas was free to betray, the judges were free to misjudge, but they could not prevent the effect of their evil deed, viz., the Crucifixion, being used by God as the means of our redemption.

St. Peter spoke of it as an evil deed, as known and permitted by God. . . . ([See] Acts 2:22-24.)

The evil which God permits must not be judged by its immediate effects, but rather by its ultimate effects. When you go to a theatre, you do not walk out because you see a good man suffering in the first act. You give the dramatist credit for a plot. Why can not you do that much with God?

— From *Go to Heaven*

Reflection

Life is filled with disappointments. It never goes quite according to our plan. People let us down; some even commit evil acts against us that seem to live on forever in our lives. There is a great danger here and Bishop Sheen in this passage helps us to understand that there is a bigger plan, and that for the person who believes in God, evil is not the final answer.

The bishop recalls the story of Joseph, the son of Jacob, found in the Book of Genesis.

Joseph had a dream that his brothers were bowing down before him. He tells them about his dream and it fills them with rage. They plot his death, but at the last second decide rather to sell him into slavery. Joseph continues his life now as a slave and wins great favor in the house of Potiphar, one of Pharaoh's officers. But when he rejects the seductions of Potiphar's wife, she turns on him and he is arrested and thrown into prison. Joseph spends his time in prison until finally a day of liberation comes when he interprets the dreams of Pharaoh relating to the future of Egypt. Now Pharaoh puts Joseph in charge of his household.

Time passes and the brothers of Joseph come to Egypt looking for food. They enter into the courts of Pharaoh and encounter Joseph (whom they do not recognize) and fall prostrate before him. Joseph leaves the room weeping. His dream has been fulfilled.

Notice how the dream that God had planted in Joseph's heart as a child is fulfilled. Much evil is done to him, but each act leads to his ultimately being where God wants him to be.

At the end of the Joseph story the brothers approach him asking for forgiveness. He tells them that what they did they meant for evil but God meant for good for the salvation of many.

The evil done to us in our lives ought not be the final definition that we give ourselves. Rather, we should remember that God has planted a dream within each of us that evil cannot destroy unless we allow something or someone other than God to guide our lives.

✝ ✝ ✝

Spend some time reflecting on one of the following:

1. Read through the story of Joseph in Genesis 37-50. What evil that has been done to you in your life do you need to let go of?

2. Using the story of Joseph found in Genesis 37-50, what is the dream that God has planted in your heart? Do you fall for the temptation that any human can destroy God's ability to bring that dream to fulfillment? Could your life be like that of Joseph's?

3. Is forgiveness weakness? Does Joseph seem weak when he forgives his brothers? Does Jesus seem weak when He forgives His executioners from the cross? Ask God for the grace to be courageous enough to forgive.

Prayer

Lord, help me to discover your will for me. Help me to forgive all who have harmed me by giving me a deep knowledge of how far your power surpasses that of any evil that can be done to me in this life. Amen.

9
The Redemption Is Reciprocal

*Now I rejoice in my sufferings for your sake, and in
my flesh I complete what is lacking in Christ's affliction
for the sake of his body, that is, the church.*
— COLOSSIANS 1:24 (RSV)

✠

Bishop Sheen

The redemption is reciprocal. Our Lord does not do
everything and we nothing. The truth is between these
extremes. The Oriental philosophy generally makes God
do everything and man nothing. Our modern Western
humanism makes man do everything and God nothing.
Christianity reveals that we are called in some way to
prolong His Life, Death, and Resurrection in our lives,
because of our solidarity with Him. It is evident then
that faith alone in the redemption of our Lord is not
sufficient to save us. Faith is important because it marks
our first disposition toward salvation. But "faith without
good works is dead." Man must respond to the first steps
God has taken, for which God justifies him, binding
him to do good works in His name. The death of our
Lord on the Cross, then, instead of dispensing us from
dying, obliges us to do so. . . .

We are not merely to copy the example of Christ
as we might copy the example of a great man, for
that would touch only the surface of the soul. Rather

are we to "put on Christ" and be possessed of His Spirit. . . .

Putting on Christ or living His mind is a long cry from any sentimental or external imitation. We are called to be conformed to Christ in all the details of His Life. He is our Saviour, but our Saviour by Sacrifice. But His Mystical Body can have no other law than His, for He is its Head. Therefore it is incumbent upon every Christian to share in His Sacrifice; to realize in time what is implied on the Cross; to actualize in our own day what was procured for us on Good Friday. He, the glorious Christ reigning at the right hand of the Father, can never again suffer in His own human nature "knowing that Christ rising again from the dead, dieth no more, (Romans 6:9)." He therefore has willed to prolong His loving Passion unto the end of the world by perpetuating it in the members of His Mystical Body who if they suffer with Him will reign with Him.

— From *The Mystical Body of Christ*

Reflection

Most of us project onto others this share in the Lord's passion. We reason that it is the saints who are called to make great sacrifices and to make great acts of charity. But we forget that we are called to be saints, and nothing less.

Virginia Cyr was born in 1942. At the age of four she began to manifest signs of cerebral palsy. Her mother, unable to handle the thought of raising the young girl in this condition, fled the home, leaving the handicapped child with her father. Due to work obligations, Virginia's father was forced to place her in a foster home and later an orphanage. One might expect that Virginia would have been bitter, but nothing could have been further from the truth.

Rather, Virginia accepted a mission that she felt Jesus had given her: to suffer with Him on the cross from the day of her birth. She was true to that mission for the rest of her short life, which was spent in various institutions throughout the State of Indiana until her death at the age of twenty-four.

She wrote in her diary, "When I was a baby, not even a day old, my loving Father in heaven tapped me on the shoulder and asked me if I'd like to do something special for Him. I was bursting with enthusiasm, and in my timid, baby way, I accepted the challenge. And what a challenge it was, and is, bringing disappointments, but far outnumbered by physical and spiritual joys."

We are all handicapped with Original Sin, but if we believe that Our Lord has saved us from that sin, then we too have a mission. Bishop Sheen reminds us that this mission is a share in Our Lord's salvific work. We will find our cross waiting for us wherever we find an excuse rising to our lips.

+ + +

Spend some time reflecting on the following:

1. What might I do for Christ today? Whose life can I touch with the love of God?

2. Read Psalm 139. Ask the Lord to reveal to you why he formed you in your mother's womb and brought you into existence knowing full well everything you would do in your life, both the good and the bad.

3. Spend some silent time in the Presence of the Lord, allowing the Lord to speak to you in your heart.

Prayer

Lord, show me each day what I can do to extend your Kingdom to all that I meet. Give me the strength to carry my cross and to follow you. Amen.

10
The Sanctification of the Present Moment

Behold, now is the acceptable time;
behold, now is the day of salvation.
— 2 CORINTHIANS 6:2 (RSV)

Bishop Sheen

Our Lord laid down the rule for us in these words: "Do not fret, then, over tomorrow; leave tomorrow to fret over its own needs; for today, today's troubles are enough." (Matt. 6:34) This means that each day has its own trials; we are not to borrow troubles from tomorrow, because that day, too, will have its cross. We are to leave the past to Divine Mercy and to trust in the future, whatever its trials, to His Loving Providence. Each minute of life has its peculiar duty — regardless of the appearance that minute may take. The Now-moment is the moment of salvation. Each complaint against it is a defeat; each act of resignation to it is a victory.

The moment is always an indication to us of God's will. The ways of pleasing Him are made clear to us in several ways: through His Commandments, by the events of His Incarnate Life in Jesus Christ Our Lord, in the Voice of His Mystical Body, the Church, in the duties of our state of life. And, in a more particular way, God's will is manifested for us in the Now with all its attendant circumstances, duties and trials.

— From *Lift Up Your Heart*

Reflection

Bishop Sheen's "Now-moment" corresponds to the thinking of the great spiritual writer Jean Pierre de Caussade. In *Abandonment to Divine Providence*, Father Caussade gives the reader a sure way of knowing the will of God at any moment — by simply confronting the present moment with all its reality. It seems simple, but if we reflect for a second, most of us will find that we spend most of our lives avoiding the present moment.

A few years ago an English translation of Father Caussade's work, with the original title changed to *The Sacrament of the Present Moment*, appeared in the United States. This captures the essence of Father Caussade's work and Bishop Sheen's meditation that in the present time we are presented with an opportunity that is truly unique. Each moment is sacramental.

Most of us are capable of presenting ourselves with some amount of reflection as we celebrate the sacraments. If we celebrated the sacrament of Baptism as an adult, certainly we came expecting to be changed by God. Each time we enter a confessional, surely we have examined our conscience beforehand and are penitent, expecting to be forgiven by God. Undoubtedly every time we approach the altar to receive the Eucharist we expect to encounter God. But what about the other moments of our lives?

As we awake in the morning, is our first thought of God? As we greet our brothers and sisters throughout the day, do we expect that God might be present? Every moment of our lives is an opportunity to encounter God, who is always present.

+ + +

Spend some time reflecting on the following:

1. Go over the events of the present day and ask yourself where God might have been in each of them. Is there a consistent pattern to your day?

2. Reflect on the life of your favorite saint, and meditate on how he or she dealt with the people the saint met in his or her daily journeys. How could you imitate this saint? What enabled the saint to act in the way he or she did toward others?

3. Imagine as you leave from this time of prayer that God wishes to continue to be present to you as you go forth. How will you react to His presence in others?

Prayer

Lord, help me to search for you in the garden of life in the same way that St. Mary Magdalene did when she found your tomb empty. May my search be rewarded as hers was by knowledge of your abiding presence. Amen.

II.

Our Lord Asks for Our Companionship

Then he said to them, "My soul is very sorrowful, even to death; remain here, and watch with me."
— MATTHEW 26:38 (RSV)

Our Lord's invitation to come into His presence and to spend time with Him demands an answer from us. Bishop Sheen gave this as the second reason to make a holy hour because Our Lord asked for our companionship. Lovers desire each other's presence; it is no different with God who loves us.

The following passages from Bishop Sheen's writings will help us to meditate on this friendship with Our Lord. All of the issues that can keep us from Him are touched upon. Sometimes we feel unworthy to be His friend; sometimes we are willing to see Him as a friend in the Eucharist but reject Him when He comes as a stranger, the sick, the hungry, or the imprisoned.

Through these meditations and prayers Bishop Sheen shows us that it is important to be a companion to Christ no matter how He chooses to come to us and above all to see that we are called to accept His grace, which makes this acceptance possible in the first place.

II
Come and See

He said to them, "Come and see."
They came and saw where he was staying;
and they stayed with him that day, ...
— JOHN 1:39 (RSV)

Bishop Sheen

Where is His permanent Presence? Where His dwelling? We know His Power is in the mountains; His Wisdom in the laws of nature; His Love in gravitation pulling all things to a center. But this is not presence. These are but effects. But Body, Blood, Soul and Divinity — "Where dost Thou live?"

We know the answer in theory. He dwells in the Eucharist. But in practice, do we know it? All that requires a search, an extra effort, maybe an hour to find out. That is why in answer to their question, He answered: "Come and see."

The "come" is a visit; to "see" is to enjoy. The first words that fell from the lips of Him Who is the Bread of Life were an invitation to seek greater union with Him. John and Andrew called Him "Master" when they first saw Him, but now they were urged to discover that He was the "Lord." At the Last Supper, He was still "Master" to Judas, but to the others, He was "Lord."

From that day to this, first-hand knowledge of Him as Lord is given to [those] who "come and see." [We] can follow, like John and Andrew. Eucharistic devotion is something added, something extra, something special in the understanding of Our Lord. One can know all the theology of the Lamb of God and Redemption, and still not walk that "extra" mile to know where He "dwells." To "come" demands leaving the [home] or the magazine; to "see" requires being in His Presence. But once before His tabernacle we can say with Job [42:5]: "I have heard Thy Voice now; nay, more, I have had sight of Thee."

A newly ordained French priest received a visit from a strange priest of another nationality. The visitor being unkempt, he was given a poor room in the attic. The French priest lived to see that visitor canonized, as Don Bosco. On learning of the canonization, he reflected: "If I [had known] he was a saint, I would have given him a better room." What will be our thoughts on the day of judgment when we reflect on the thousands of times we passed our church or a chapel without even a quick prayer, a greeting? The innkeeper at Bethlehem did not "see" that it was He. The capitalists of the Gerasenes did not know it was He. The Samaritans, who refused to receive Him, did not know it was He.

Now as we ask the question: "Where dost Thou dwell?" He points to the tabernacle and says, "Come and see." We should do ill not to love Him when He brings Himself so close.

— From *The Priest Is Not His Own*

Reflection

Our Lord reveals to us what God is like. It is easy to reduce God to a foreign impersonal object that is distant and does not concern itself with infinitesimal specks that we must appear to be to the Almighty. But Revelation teaches us that God chose to become a speck like us and to dwell among us. What is more, He had friends and sought their companionship.

Bishop Sheen reminds us in this passage that Our Lord desires our company. Jesus reveals God as a personal God, someone that desires a relationship with His people. We may say that we have a relationship with God, but do we spend time in His presence? If you have picked up this book as an aid to prayer in His presence, then of course you do.

But if you have picked it up in a bookstore out of curiosity and turned to this page, you might find the idea novel. God desires my company? Why not? Do we have close friends who do not desire our company? Do we have a loved one who never wishes to be with us?

Jesus has revealed God as Emmanuel, "God with us." To the question that rises in every believer's heart, "Where is God?" Jesus answers, "Come and see."

Bishop Sheen applies this to the Eucharistic Presence of Our Lord. I remember hearing a talk once given by the archbishop in which he invited anyone who doubted the Real Presence of Our Lord to go into a Catholic church and spend one hour in silence alone with the Blessed Sacrament.

That person would not be alone in that Church.

Our Lord seeks our companionship and we know where He is to be found.

+ + +

Spend some time reflecting on the following:

1. What opportunities do you have to visit Our Lord in your daily life? Do you speak to Him as someone who desires to know the secrets of your heart?

2. Open your heart before the Lord, telling Him all that is on your mind as you would your best friend. Listen for His response.

3. Mediate on John 1:39 (quoted at the beginning of the meditation). Imagine that you are present at this event. What does Jesus look like to you? Does He speak to you? What does He say?

Prayer

Lord, I have come here to see you, to be in your presence. I adore you and worship you as the one true God. Help me to love you with all my heart and always seek to be close to you. Amen.

12
Love Is Triune

"All who love the Lord God in truth and righteousness will rejoice, showing mercy to our brethren."
— Tobit 14:7 (RSV)

Bishop Sheen

The basic error of mankind has been to assume that only two are needed for love: you and me, or society and me, or humanity and me.

Really it takes three: self, other selves, and God; you, and me, and God. Love of self without love of God is selfishness; love of neighbor without love of God embraces only who are pleasing to us, not those who are hateful. One cannot tie two sticks together without something outside the sticks; one cannot bind the nations of the world except by the recognition of a Law and a Person outside the nations themselves. Duality in love is extinction through exhaustion of self-giving. Love is triune or it dies. It requires three virtues, faith, hope, and charity, which intertwine, purify, and regenerate each other. To believe in God is to throw ourselves into His arms; to hope in Him is to rest in His heart in patience amidst trials and tribulations; to love Him is to be with Him through a participation of His Nature through grace. If love did not have faith and trust, it would die; if love did not have hope, its sufferings would be torture, and love might seem loveless. Love of self, of neighbor, and love of God go together and when separated fall apart.

Love of self without love of God is egotism, for if there is no Perfect Love from Whom we came and for Whom we are destined, then the ego becomes the center. But when self is loved in God, the whole concept of what is self-perfection changes. If the ego is an absolute, its perfection consists in having whatever will make it happy, and at all costs; this is the essence of egotism, or selfishness. If union with Perfect Love is the goal of personality, then its perfection consists not in having but in being had, not in owning but in being owned, or better still, not in having but in being.

Union with Perfect Happiness or God is not something extrinsic to us, like a gold medal to a student, but is, rather, intrinsic to our nature, as blooming is to a flower. Without it we are unsatisfied and incomplete.

— From *Three to Get Married*

Reflection

In this passage, Bishop Sheen points out a truth that is the perfect test to see whether our spiritual lives are of God or ourselves. The test is this: Do we see our spiritual obligation involving three: God, my neighbor, and myself?

Some people can focus on God at the expense of everyone else including themselves. Clearly this is not what Jesus revealed a spiritual person to be. Some act as though helping others is to be done at the expense of any prayer time or any care for themselves. Again this is not what Jesus revealed. Finally there are those who pray to God and help their neighbor but have contempt for themselves. We were created by God and are special to Him. How could anyone ever have contempt for oneself knowing that he or she is loved by God?

These three pseudo-spiritualities are shown for what they are in the light of the Holy Trinity: Father, Son, and Holy Spirit. God has revealed Himself as a community of love, and everything that He has brought into existence shares the essence of His being.

Do we need to pray more? Do we need to reach out to others more? Do we need to take heed of what our mission in life is? All these things are important if we are to be the person God has created us to be.

+ + +

Spend some time reflecting on the following:

1. How much do you love God? What acts do you daily do that show your love for God? What more could you do? Ask God for the grace to love Him more.

2. How much do you love the people who surround you? Are there people you need to ask forgiveness from? Could you do more to help others? Ask God for the grace to love others.

3. How much do you love yourself? Have you accepted God's definition of who you are? Or do

you allow others to define you? Ask God for the grace to know yourself as He has created you.

Prayer

Lord God, Father, Son, and Holy Spirit, help us to grow spiritually so that our actions may reflect a greater love toward you, the people around us, and ourselves. Amen.

13
Tragic Words

*He came unto his own, and his
own received him not.*
— JOHN 1:11 (*Douay-Rheims*)

✠

Bishop Sheen

The most tragic words ever written of Our Lord are those which John sets down in the beginning of his Gospel: "He came unto His own and His own received Him not." Bethlehem had no room for Him when He was born; Nazareth no room for Him while He lived, Jerusalem no room for Him when He died.

What happened then is happening today. The curtain never goes down on the great abiding drama of Calvary. In every century the same leading role is played by the Eternal Galilean, but new characters play the other roles. The story is always the same: the age-old story of indifference struck on a new key, in new hearts, and in new times. He still brings salvation, but men are indifferent to being saved. He still brings healing grace, but men are indifferent to their ills. He still comes into His own, but His own receive Him not.

— From *The Eternal Galilean*

Reflection

Once while attending Mass at the National Shrine of the North American Martyrs, I heard the Jesuit priest who was presiding at the liturgy preach on the Gospel for that day, which was from John 1:12 — "He came to what was his own, but his own people did not accept him." His homily was simple, but one that I have not forgotten ten years later.

The priest simply repeated John 1:12 and said with great emotion, "What a tragedy!"

While preparing the selections for this book I was surprised to find exactly the same wording in Bishop Sheen's writings. Obviously the priest had either read or heard the archbishop and it had left an impression upon him.

Bishop Sheen was able to personalize the Gospel in his preaching and writing. In this passage he does so by planting the encounter with Our Lord not in the past but in the events of the present moment. How will we respond to the invitation of Jesus? When He comes to us in the Eucharist, will we respond by accepting the invitation or will we reject it?

+ + +

Spend some time reflecting on the following:

1. How is the Lord inviting you to be with Him today? Have you accepted His coming to you today in the Eucharist? What about in the hungry, the stranger, the sick, or the imprisoned?

2. Reflect on those who say "no" to the Lord's invitation. Pray for them, asking the Lord to give them the grace to say "yes" to His love.

3. Meditate on the tragic response of those who refuse to accept the Lord's gracious invitation. Pray for the grace to have a clear sense of the tragedy in saying no to God ever.

Prayer

Lord, I accept your invitation. Thank you for coming into my presence today both in the Holy Eucharist and in the many people that will cross my path this day. May I welcome each of them as you. Amen.

14
A Word to Sinners

"Jesus, remember me when you come into your kingdom."
— LUKE 23:42 (NAB)

✠

Bishop Sheen

There are two ways of coming to God: through the preservation of innocence; and through the loss of it. Some have come to God because they were good, like Mary, who was "full of grace"; like Joseph, the "just man"; like Nathaniel, *"in* whom there was no guile"; or like John the Baptist, "the greatest man ever born of woman."

But others have come to God who were bad, like the young man of the Gerasenes "possessed of devils"; like Magdalen, out of whose corrupt soul the Lord cast seven devils; and like the thief at the right who spoke the second word to the Cross.

The world loves the mediocre. The world hates the very good and the very bad. The good are a reproach to the mediocre, and the evil are a disturbance. That is why Christ was crucified with thieves. Seven hundred years before, Isaias had prophesied that He would be "reputed with the wicked" *(Isaias* 53:12). Luke verified it: "And with the wicked was he reckoned" *(Luke* 22:37).

So it was willed by God. This is His true position: Jesus among the worthless ones. During His life He was accused of eating and drinking with sinners; now they can accuse Him of dying with them. And these companions on their crosses were not political prisoners, nor castoff capitalists from a proletarian revolution; they were just plain bandits — pure and simple.

Here is a supreme instance of the Right Man in the right place: Christ among the bandits; the redeemer in the midst of the unredeemed; the Physician among the lepers — for God does not work through culture but through grace. He does not ask men to be refined; He asks them to be penitent. Thus does God show that we become great not because of what we are, but because of what He gives.

— From *Seven Words to the Cross*

Reflection

There is sometimes a reluctance among older Catholics to think that God would have anything to do with them if they have sinned. As young children, many of them had been burdened with a fear that they would die before making it to the confessional on a Saturday afternoon.

This deep sense of sin may have been lost on a younger generation. But the truth lies between the two extremes. Sin grieves God, but He always loves us even when we have sinned. He seeks our companionship constantly.

Several years ago, when a serial murderer was being electrocuted for his crimes a reporter interviewed the mother of the man. He wondered what she felt toward her son who had committed such heinous acts against a number of men and women. She said that she hated that her son had done such horrible things and wasted his life but she emphasized that she still loved him.

God has revealed that His love is no different. We are His creation and He loves us no matter how terrible our sins have been or how we have wasted His gifts. His desire remains the same: that we come to Him and accept His love.

Bishop Sheen's message was that there are only thieves in heaven — which is true to a degree, since God's love is so generous and we are so ungrateful that an objective viewer of our situation could only see us as thieves, stealing from a God who loves us so much.

✝   ✝   ✝

Spend some time reflecting on the following:

1. In Scripture, Satan is called the accuser. Do you allow Satan's accusations against you to keep you from feeling God's love and desire for your companionship in your life?

2. Do you allow your sins to keep you from God? Are there sins that you have not confessed out of pride? Ask God for the grace for perfect contrition for your sins.

3. Meditate on those crucified beside Jesus. Both were thieves: one repented, the other did not. Pray the words of the good thief, "Jesus, remember me when you come into your kingdom."

Prayer

Lord, teach me to love you more and to see all sin as a rejection of your love. Fill me with a grace to desire nothing but your love and to always live in your peace. Amen.

15
Hope

"Truly, I say to you, today you will be with me in Paradise."
— LUKE 23:43 (RSV)

✠

Bishop Sheen

Our concern presently is with two kinds of souls; the despairing and the presumptuous: either those who say, "I am too wicked for God to be interested in me," or those who say, "Oh, I need not worry about my sins. God will take good care of me in the end."

Both these statements are sins of exaggeration. The first is the sin of despair which exaggerates Divine Justice; the second is the sin of presumption which exaggerates Divine Mercy. Somewhere there is a golden mean where "Justice and mercy kiss" as the Psalmist puts it, and that is the virtue of Hope.

The *virtue* of Hope is quite different from the *emotion* of Hope. The emotion centers in the body and is a kind of dreamy desire that we can be saved without much effort. The virtue of Hope, however, is centered in the *will* and may be defined as a divinely infused disposition of the will by which with sure confidence, thanks to the powerful help of Almighty God, we expect to pursue eternal happiness, using all the means necessary for attaining it.

The virtue of Hope lies not in the future of time, but beyond the tomb in eternity; its object is not the abundant life of earth, but the eternal love of God.

— From *The Seven Virtues*

Reflection

Bishop Sheen presents us with two extremes that can plague us in our relationship with Our Lord: despair and presumption.

Those who despair, focus on themselves to such a degree that they do not realize how much greater God's love and mercy are than any sin or offense that they are capable of committing against Him. The evil of despair is that the person who may feign humility is really the proudest of people who believes that his or her sins are too great for even God to forgive. The despair that such a soul feels is a wall that never allows God's forgiveness to permeate the person's soul and be freed from the chains of egoism.

Those who are presumptuous, on the other hand, are an uncaring sort who treat their relationship with God as if God were indifferent to whether or not they destroy their lives by the choices made. Such individuals keep God in their back pocket as a lucky charm with no real concern in their lives other than to manipulate their genie god.

The true companions of Our Lord are different. They neither take for granted their good fortune of having so great a savior nor do they fear that He will let them down; rather, they are moved through whatever experiences come their way with a fervent hope that in the end they will be with Him.

As in the present moment, so in eternity. We are always in God's presence. There is no place one can go to escape it. The person who prays in the presence of the Blessed Sacrament is made aware of God's presence in a unique way and indeed is privileged with a foretaste of heaven.

+ + +

Spend some time reflecting on the following:

1. Reflect on those who despair. Why is this not a holy act? Does a person who despairs really believe in a merciful God? Ask God for the grace to always trust in His mercy.

2. Reflect on the sin of presumption. Why is it wrong to presume on God's mercy? Ask God for the grace to see that His will is truly merciful and any time we choose other than His will we are worshiping something or someone else.

3. Reflect on the virtue of hope. What areas of your life could use this virtue? Do you trust in the companionship of Our Lord? Do you have assurance that He loves you and wishes for you to be with Him for all eternity? Ask for this grace.

Prayer

Lord, send your Holy Spirit to fill me with the virtue of hope. Open my eyes to the eternal reward that awaits all of your friends. Help me to do your will in this life and to always be focused on your service. Amen.

16
The Divine Embrace

*God is love, and he who abides in love abides
in God, and God abides in him.*
— 1 JOHN 4:16 (RSV)

✠

Bishop Sheen

A young wife, who had been taking instructions for a
year, told the writer she could believe everything in
the faith except the Eucharist. Upon inquiring about
her husband, it was learned that he was in the Pacific
on military duty. In answer to further questions, she
admitted that she corresponded with him every two
days and that she had his photograph before her in
the house.

We argued there was nothing wanting for perfect
happiness. What more could she want than the constant memory of him through the photograph and a
written communication in which heart poured out
to heart? But she protested that she could never be
truly happy except through union with her husband.

But, it was retorted, if human love craves oneness,
shall not divine love? If husband and wife seek to be
one in the flesh, shall not the Christian and Christ
crave for that oneness with one another? The memory
of the Christ who lived twenty centuries ago, the
recalling of His mercy and miracles through memory,

the correspondence with Him by reading the Scriptures — all these are satisfying, but they do not satisfy love. There must be, on the level of grace, something unitive with divine love. Every heart seeks a happiness outside it, and since perfect love is God, then the heart of man and the heart of Christ must, in some way, fuse. In human friendship the other person is loved as another self, or the other half of one's soul. Divine friendship must have its mutual "indwelling": "He who dwells in love dwells in God and God in him" (I John 4:16). This aspiration of the soul for its ecstasy is fulfilled in the Sacrament of the Eucharist.

— From *These Are the Sacraments*

Reflection

The first effect of the Eucharist is that it unites us with Our Lord in a way that is so complete that we can say with St. Paul, "It is no longer I who live, but Christ who lives in me" (Galatians 2:20, RSV). This is so great a gift that it behooves us to meditate often on this union as we pray in the Lord's presence. The Lord is indeed within us, but do we allow Him to rule our lives?

St. Paul, in his Second Letter to the Corinthians, presents us with a test, one that could be fruitful during this period of prayer. He tells the Corinthians and, by extension, us: "Examine yourselves, to see whether you are holding to your faith. Test yourselves. Do you not realize that Jesus Christ is in you?" (2 Corinthians 13:5, RSV).

As Bishop Sheen points out, Our Lord seeks an intimacy with us so complete that He wishes to become one with us. The intimacy of a married couple can produce a new life, and so can intimacy with God. With God, the new life is our very self.

St. Paul's test is a simple one, one that asks us to realize what has happened to our very being.

We may fall prey to the temptation that we are not worthy of so great a love (and we are not) or that something can separate us from this love. We look to St. Paul again: "Who shall separate us from the love of Christ? Shall tribulation, or distress, or persecution, or famine, or nakedness, or peril, or sword?" (Romans 8:35, RSV).

The answer? "No, in all these things we are more than conquerors through him who loved us. For I am sure that neither death, nor life, nor angels, nor principalities, nor things present, nor things to come, nor powers, nor height, nor depth, nor anything else in all creation, will be able to separate us from the love of God in Christ Jesus our Lord" (Romans 8:37-39, RSV).

+ + +

Spend some time reflecting on the following:

1. Reflect on St. Paul's words that "it is no longer I who live, but Christ who lives in me" (Galatians 2:20). Do you experience your relationship with Our Lord in this way? Ask God for the grace to have a greater sense of the union that Jesus desires to have with you.

2. Reflect on what St. Paul means when he says, "Have among yourselves the same attitude that is also yours in Christ Jesus" (Philippians 2:5, NAB). Do you have the same attitudes in life as Our Lord? Ask Him for this grace.

3. Reflect on 1 John 4:16, "God is love, and he who abides in love abides in God, and God abides in him" (RSV). Do you find that your relationship with Our Lord immerses you in love and overflows into the other activities of your day? Ask God for the grace to be made perfect in love.

Prayer

Lord, fill me with your love. Help me have your mind in all that I think, say, and do. When I receive the Eucharist, make me aware of my Holy Communion with you. Amen.

17
The Effects of the Eucharist

*"He who eats my flesh and drinks my blood
abides in me, and I in him."*
— JOHN 6:56 (RSV)

✠

Bishop Sheen

The Eucharist not only sets a value on man by making it possible for him to commune with God, but it also makes it possible for man to commune with his fellow man. The first effect of the Eucharist is personal; the second effect is communal and social, inasmuch as the soul is introduced not only to its Maker, but to his brother, in that fellowship of the saints, and organized society of spiritual units where the integrating principle is Love. The point here is to suggest how the Eucharist is the Bond of Fellowship. An example will make it clear: What the blood plasma is to the human body, that of the Eucharist is to the Mystical Body. In the human body is a lymph flowing through the bloodstream, carrying a store of provisions which is tapped by each individual cell; supplying it not only with the food it needs, but also repairing its waste parts. This flowing tide of sustenance passes by every door, displaying and offering its goods to its tiny little cells, making them all one body because all are nourished by the same food.

The Eucharist is the lymph of the Mystical Body. Like a mighty river it swells and sweeps through the Church in every part of the world, breaking its secret of salvation to every individual Catholic, whispering its wonderful message of love for the healing of wounds to this one, dipping the chalice of its wine for the increase of joy to that one, thus making them all one because nourished by the same Bread. Such is the meaning of the words of St. Paul: "All who eat the one Bread are one Body." This is the Christian foundation for the social order, for international peace, for brotherly love — unity in Christ Jesus, our Lord.

— From *The Cross and the Crisis*

Reflection

The second effect of the Eucharist Bishop Sheen states is both communal and social. The reception of Our Lord into our lives affects the way we see others and the way we treat them as well.

There was a story told by a priest that I heard some years ago about an experience he had as a young boy. He had the habit of serving Benediction on Friday evenings following the Stations of the Cross in his parish. And it had become so routine that on this particular night he found his mind was wandering. The other boy serving with him, whom he described as fat, kept nodding off. He nudged the boy, who, startled, let out a yelp. Of course this caught the priest's attention, and he directed a stern look toward his servers.

In the midst of all these distractions, the young server noticed the Blessed Sacrament in the monstrance. At that moment, it was as if a voice came from the host saying, "I'm more than just a host, you know."

When he looked over at the altar boy serving with him to see if he too had heard the voice, he was surprised to find the voice emanating from the boy, "I'm more than just a fat altar boy, you know."

Then later that night as he left the church, over and over again from every person he encountered, "I'm more than whatever you think of me, you know."

Our encounter with Jesus in the Blessed Sacrament should affect us in a similar way. When we leave this chapel with the mind and attitude of Christ, we will find that each person we meet is much more than whatever we personally think of that individual.

+   +   +

Spend some time reflecting upon the following:

1. How does your devotion to Our Lord change the way you view others? Are there people that you cannot see as having any value? Place whomever the Lord brings to your mind in prayer before Him, praying for that person's needs and that God's will be done in his or her life.

2. Do you experience both effects of the Eucharist, the personal and the social? Ask God for the grace to deepen this experience of His communion with you.

3. Reflect on the Mystical Body of Christ. What does it mean that we are all members and Christ is the head? Do you experience others as having a meaningful role to play in the salvation of the world?

Prayer

Lord, enable me to see in my brothers and sisters what you see in them. Unite me with your love and empower me to share that love with all I meet this day. Amen.

18
Mortification: Dying to Live

*"Lord, to whom shall we go? You have the words
of eternal life; and we have believed, and have come
to know, that you are the Holy One of God."*
— JOHN 6:68-69 (RSV)

Bishop Sheen

It is one of the curious anomalies of present-day civilization that when man achieves greatest control over nature, he has the least control over himself. The great boast of our age is our domination of the universe: we have harnessed the waterfalls, made the wind a slave to carry us on wings of steel, and squeezed from the earth the secret of its age. Yet, despite this mastery of nature, there perhaps never was a time when man was less a master of himself. He is equipped like a veritable giant to control the forces of nature, but is as weak as a pigmy to control the forces of his passions and inclinations.

If, indeed, this life is a vale of character making, and if it involves conflict with those forces and powers which would drag us away from our ideals, then it behooves us to realize that the truest conquest is self-conquest, that true progress may more properly consist in mastering our rampant impulses and selfish desires, than in mastering the winds and seas. But this conquest of self cannot be attained except by a struggle which in Christian language is mortification. Mortification means dying to live for the love of God.

— From *The Moral Universe*

Reflection

Our Lord invited His followers to take up their cross and to follow Him. But notice that this act of self-renunciation is not a solitary act. Rather, it is an act by which we join the Lord on the path to Calvary. We become His companions on a journey that He has already trod before us.

Bishop Sheen presents us with two types of people. There are those who are living to die, and then there are those who are dying to live.

Those who are living to die are focused on getting everything that they can out of the few precious moments of existence that they have on this earth. The modern conveniences have made it easier for them to cram even more pleasure into their short lives.

But there are others who have come to the realization that this earthly life is not all there is but only a beginning. These see each moment as an opportunity to invest in the future of eternity. They forgo pleasure in order to do good for others. They constantly search for where the Lord might be found in the present moment. Like an expectant mother, the trials of the present are bearable for the joy to come.

+ + +

Spend some time reflecting on the following:

1. How have you answered the Lord's call to take up your cross and follow Him? Is there an area of your life that the Lord is calling you to practice mortification in? What do you need to die to in your life?

2. Meditate on the state of humanity in the twenty-first century and all the advances that humans have made in the past hundred years. How do these advances affect your relationship with God?

3. Reflect on Our Lord fasting in the desert for forty days and forty nights. Why did He, the Son of God, do this? What does Jesus' practice teach you about mortification?

Prayer

Lord, keep my eyes focused on you as you carry your cross before me. Help me to see that whatever burdens I bear on this journey with you are light because you are there to share the weight of them. Amen.

19
Meditation

Bishop Sheen

Though many of our contemporary writers are correct in protesting against the mere indoctrination of truth which is never lived out, they have generally failed to offer the one means most calculated to make knowledge relevant and personal, and that is by meditation. Meditation acts on man somewhat the same as functional medicine. Not long ago, doctors were so specialized that they treated only diseases and not sick people. Now medical practitioners affirm the necessity of treating the whole person. In like manner, it is only by meditation that one personalizes a truth.

Taking an example from Buddhism: A student is supposed to so meditate on the bull's-eye he will shoot with arrows that, after many hours of practice and meditation, he can not only hit the target with his eyes closed, but he can also make the second arrow hit the first arrow which hit the center of the target.

The concentration of the student is on the target, and not just on the bow and arrow.

Meditation generally is considered as a reflection on something that one seizes and makes part of oneself, for example the compassion of Our Lord in feeding the hungry multitude. Meditation, rather, is not merely thinking of compassion outside of oneself, but also trying to think oneself into compassion and mercy and kindness. Here one touches on the great difference between German and Oriental mystics on the one hand, and the great Spanish mystics on the other. The former were satisfied to be absorbed into Divinity, but the Spanish mystics, among whom the greatest was St. Teresa, tended to absorb the Deity into themselves. St. Teresa wrote:

> *This Divine union of love in which I live*
> *Makes God my captive and my heart free.*
> *But it causes me such pain to see God my prisoner*
> *That I die of longing to die.*

Here there is a flaming dart plunged into the saint's passionate breast through her meditation.

One may give a thousand lectures on the chemical composition of water to a swimmer, but there is nothing like plunging into the Mediterranean and feeling the warm water buoy him up and quicken his spirit.

How different our lives would become if we would take an hour a day not to think about the attributes of God and the moral law, but to make the love of God and the love of neighbor experientially present in our own heart and soul! Man does not want to be with God as much as God wants to be with man. This is the secret of meditation. Try it and be happy.

— From *Fulton J. Sheen's Guide to Contentment*

Reflection

A traditional image of Our Lord's presence in the Blessed Sacrament is that He is there as a prisoner of love. I recall a prayer book that even portrayed this by showing that where a monstrance and the Blessed Sacrament would normally be, instead were prison bars and behind them Our Blessed Lord looking out in hopeful expectation of someone coming to visit Him soon.

God desires our companionship, but He does not force Himself upon us. Rather He waits for us to come to Him. When Our Lord rose from the dead, His angel instructed the women to tell the disciples to go to Galilee and there they would see Him. He would not force Himself on them; rather, He wanted them to come to Him.

It has not changed. He still waits for us.

Bishop Sheen in this passage urges us to experience this reality by practicing Christian meditation. We reflect on Our Lord's life until we become so united with the events of that life that we experience them in the present. That can begin now as we meditate on how Our Lord has chosen to be present with us.

+ + +

Spend some time reflecting on the following:

1. Reread the verse written by St. Teresa, quoted in the passage from Bishop Sheen above. Ask God for the grace to feel His presence within your heart.

2. Meditate on the Last Supper. See how Our Lord humbles Himself to avail us of His presence. Ask God for the grace to let go of the sin of pride in your life.

3. Pray for an increase of love in your heart both for God and your neighbor. Ask Jesus to touch your heart with His nail-pierced hands and to open your heart to His abundant grace.

Prayer

Lord, help me to meditate on your life in a way that inspires me to live as you did. Give me the grace necessary to love you and my neighbor more and more each day. Amen.

20
Brotherhood

And all who believed were together and had all things in common; and they sold their possessions and goods and distributed them to all, as any had need.
— ACTS 2:44-45 (RSV)

Bishop Sheen

It should be evident that the sharing of economic wealth will not make us brothers, but becoming brothers will make us share economic wealth. The early Christians were not one because they pooled their wealth; they pooled their wealth because they were Christians.

The rich young man went to Our Lord asking: "What shall *I* do?" The Socialist asks: "What shall *society* do?" It is man who makes society and not society which makes man. That is why all the economic schemes from Marx's Communism to the latest form of Democratic Collectivism will never unite men until they have first learned to burn, purge and cut away their own selfishness.

The "One World" will not come at the end of an ascending line of progress, but as the Resurrection from a tomb of a thousand crucified egotisms.

The reason Christianity lives and Socialist theories perish is because Socialism makes no provision for getting rid of selfishness, but Our Lord did: "Sell all whatever thou hast, and give to the poor." (Luke 18:22)

The only place in the world where communism works is in a convent, for there the basis of having everything in common is that no one wants anything. Communism has not worked in Moscow, but it does work in a monastery.

All that economic and political revolutions do is shift booty and loot from one party's pocket to another. For that reason, none of them is really revolutionary: they all leave greed in the heart of man.

The true inspiration for fellowship is not law but love. Law is negative: "Thou shalt *not*." Love is positive: "*Love* God and *love* neighbor." Law is concerned with the minimum: "Speed limit, 35 miles." Love is concerned with the maximum: "Be ye perfect as your heavenly Father is perfect."

Law is for moderation; love is generous: "And if a man will contend with thee in judgment, and take away thy coat, let go thy cloak also unto him. And whosoever will force thee one mile, go with him other two." (Matthew 5:40-41)

Natural generosity is limited by circumstances and relations within our circle, and outside of these is often vindictive. Love ignores all limits, by forgiveness.

"Lord, how often shall my brother offend against me, and I forgive him? till seven times? . . . I say not to thee, till seven times; but till seventy times seven times." (Matthew 18:21-22) By moving from a little metaphor to a big one, Our Lord implies that precision in forgiveness is impossible. Leave it to love and it is not likely to err on the lower side.

The love of which we speak is not natural, but supernatural. By faith and good works under God's grace, nourished by prayer and the Sacraments, we are led into intimate union with Christ — but this love we have toward Him must redound to all His creatures.

— From *Love One Another*

Reflection

Proposed solutions to the problems that humanity faces arise every day. If we do this or that, we will solve what has seemed unsolvable before. But as Bishop Sheen remarks, these theories all pass like the ones that have come before them except one — that of Christian love.

But Christian love is not something that we decide that we will do on our own. Christian love is based on a relationship with Christ. Its power comes from Christ. Changed by the power of Christ, St. Francis was able to embrace the leper he so despised before.

Most of us recoil at the demands that the Gospel makes of us because we think of it as a human enterprise. We imagine that we would never be able to help the poor or reach out to those in need. We excuse ourselves, claiming it isn't in our nature to do these acts and instead leave them in the hands of the "saints."

We miss the point. These acts are, indeed, humanly impossible. It is only through the power of God that we can come to embrace all with the love of God. Our prayer should always be that God will transform us and empower us to do what is impossible.

Mother Teresa often surprised those who met her upon her arrival at one of her many convents throughout the world. She would often take up a broom and go into the streets and sweep. In doing so she was transforming the area.

We often think only of the immense tasks of love while ignoring the simple. Start with a smile to the passing stranger, a wave to someone that could easily be ignored. In short, start by noticing those who so often go unnoticed.

+ + +

Spend some time reflecting on the following:

1. Reread the description of the early Church found in Acts 2:44-45 (quoted at the beginning of this section). What enabled the early Christians to live like this? Ask God for the grace to fill you with a love that is giving.

2. Ask God to reveal to you any areas of selfishness that remain within you. Seek in prayer to discover what fears underlie these areas. Ask God to be rid of fears that have no basis in reality.

3. Reflect on the difference between natural love and supernatural love as Bishop Sheen describes it in the above passage. Do most of your acts reflect natu-

ral or supernatural love? Ask God to give you the grace to love like He does.

Prayer

Lord, rid us of the fears that keep us prisoners in ourselves. Help us instead to reach out to others out of love for you. Fill us with your love and give us the grace to love you more and to share that love with one another. Amen.

We Grow into the Likeness of Our Lord

*And we all, with unveiled face, beholding the glory
of the Lord, are being changed into his likeness
from one degree of glory to another; for this comes
from the Lord who is the Spirit.*
— 2 Corinthians 3:18 (RSV)

Whenever Moses had been in the presence of God,
his face shone so brightly afterward that he had to
wear a veil over it so that the people could approach
him. He himself was unaware of this change in his
appearance. We read in Exodus 34:29-30, "Moses
did not know that the skin of his face shone because
he had been talking with God. And when Aaron and
all the people of Israel saw Moses, behold, the skin
of his face shone, and they were afraid to come near
him" (RSV).

Bishop Sheen used this example from Scripture
with regard to our spending time in front of the

Blessed Sacrament. This exercise will change us. We cannot leave the presence of Our Lord without being transformed. We may be unaware of the change, but others will notice, saying, "There is something different about you."

I recently passed a church that had a sign posted out in front of it that read: "Spending time in the presence of the Son will keep you from being burned."

Our Lord wishes our eternal salvation and also wishes that we become more like Him. In these passages from Bishop Sheen we reflect on growing to be more like Our Lord.

✠

21
Christian Asceticism

And you became imitators of us and of the Lord,
for you received the word in much affliction,
with joy inspired by the Holy Spirit.
— 1 THESSALONIANS 1:6 (RSV)

Bishop Sheen

We want to be more than we are when we mortify ourselves. The only reason for dying is to discover new life. Easter must be more than a sunset on Good Friday. If we give up property, we want something more than property for our surrender. All asceticism implies elevation to a new order, a brighter life, a nobler kingdom.

Such is the philosophy of Christian asceticism. Asceticism is not a sleep. You do not go to bed to wake up to a new job. You wake up beyond the need of laboring at all. Nature itself proclaims the lesson that the death of asceticism is a birth to a higher life. Plants die in order to live in the animal; animals die to live in the kingdom of man; and man dies to himself by mortification in order to live a Godlike life in Christ. "Unless you die to yourself you cannot live in My Kingdom." In the Christian plan you die to this world to live in the next world, not to a bettered existence in this one. It is not worth passing through a revolution with its social upheaval and pillaging of tabernacles just for the sake of transferring the privilege of wealth from the envious Capitalists to the newly envious Commissars. But it is worth denying oneself all the pleasures of this world to be lifted up into an order where there is no more blood to be shed, no more brothers to hate, for all are one in God who is Peace and Love.

— From *Freedom Under God*

Reflection

Dying to our own selfish desires is a constant battle that is only won when our eyes are kept on Our Lord. We become more like Him the more we gaze upon His life and come to appropriate for ourselves the way He lived when He walked on the face of the earth.

A few years ago a popular practice among some Christians was to wear an armband embroidered with the letters WWJD. Wearing the wristband like the phylacteries worn by the ancient Jews or in the way that a scapular or miraculous medal might be worn by a Catholic was a way of constantly keeping in mind not only the presence of God but the demands of a life in Christ. The letters stood for a simple slogan: "What would Jesus do?"

Ultimately the source of mortification in our daily lives revolves around the question "What would the Lord do if He were in this situation right here and right now?"

We know that Jesus spent time in prayer. We know that Jesus brought healing wherever He went. We know that He stood up for those who were mistreated. We know that He fed the hungry. We know that He died for our sins.

What would He do if He were confronted with the problems that face your day?

It is amazing how most of us can usually answer this question rather quickly. The Lord's will and ways are not esoteric. Most of us can readily see what God asks of us, but as Bishop Sheen says in this reflection, it takes a dying to self in order to actually carry out this mission in our daily lives.

✝ ✝ ✝

Spend some time reflecting on the following:

1. Imagine Jesus living your life. What would be different? Ask for the grace to live your life as you imagine Jesus would.

2. Meditate on 1 Thessalonians 1:6 at the beginning of this section. Why are affliction and joy mixed as the expected response to be imitators of Our Lord and St. Paul? Ask the Lord to fill you with the joy that makes mortification possible.

3. Ask the Lord for the grace to become more like Him. Allow Him to tell you how you already reflect His grace and love in your life. Thank Him for the many graces He has given you in this life.

Prayer

Lord, keep your presence before me this day so that I may constantly strive to be like you in all that I do, say, and think. May every thought I have be directed toward you. Amen.

22
Silence

✠

Bishop Sheen

One of the really great needs of our own day is silence. Modern life seems to thrive on a fondness for noise, and by noise I mean not only the staccato barbarism of jazz, or the bleating and moaning of saxophone orchestras, but also, and principally, the excessive desire for that which distracts — love of amusements, constant goings and comings, excitements and thrills, and movement for the mere sake of movement. What is the reason of this fondness for noise? It is not due to any inherent love of that which is loud, for people generally prefer that which is soft and refined. Rather the reason is to be found in the great desire on the part of human beings to do the impossible, namely — to escape from themselves. They do not like to be with themselves because they are not pleased with themselves; they do not like to be alone with their conscience, because their conscience reproves and carries on an unbearable repartee. They do not like to be quiet, because the footsteps of the Hound of Heaven which can be heard in silence, cannot be heard in the din of excitement; they do not like to be silent, because God's voice is like a whisper and it cannot be heard in the tumult of the city streets. These are some of the reasons why the modern world loves noise, and they are all resolvable to this: noise drowns God's voice and stupefies conscience. Dull, indeed, are these distractions, but like the clay used by savages to dull the pain of hunger, they stifle in the soul the hunger for the presence of God. The result is that very few people ever know themselves. In fact, they know every one else better than they know themselves. That is why so few ever see their own faults. . . .

In order to remedy this condition, what is needed is less amusing and more musing; a silence; a going apart into the desert of our souls to rest a while; a solitariness from men, and an aloneness with God; a quiet which permits the soul to be sensitive to the whispers of God; a requiem or a rest from modern maxims and the excuses of new philosophies and the excitements which appeal to the body and disturb the soul; a privacy inspired by the example of Him who needed least of all mankind a preparation of silence for a life of activity, and yet had the greatest of them all; a tranquility inspired by Him who in the midst of a busy life spent whole nights on mountaintops in prayer.

Silence is the condition of entering into oneself, which is another way of saying, of finding God.

— From *Moods and Truths*

Reflection

Bishop Sheen shows that the practice of silence is in imitation of Our Lord, who spent entire nights alone in prayer. If He, the Son of God, did this, how much more do we need to do it?

We become like Our Lord when we pray because, like Him, we come to know who we are in God's eyes and what our mission is in this life. The Scriptures highlight that Jesus spent the night in prayer before choosing the twelve apostles (see Luke 6:12-13) and before His arrest and crucifixion.

We know that in His prayer at Gethsemane Jesus prayed from His heart, pouring out what was on His mind to the Father. But we also know from that same prayer that He was silent and waited for a response. An angel was sent to strengthen Our Lord in response to His waiting.

Too often we can be tempted to do all of the talking in prayer and not leave room for God to respond to us. As Bishop Sheen points out, fear is what keeps us from being silent. We are afraid of what God might reveal to us if we are silent. The Scriptures show us that this is not abnormal but that the message of God's angels is always the same: "Do not fear."

There is a great power in silence, something that is almost palpable. We notice the world around us in a way that we don't when we fill our lives with noise. This awareness leads to our being present to the now. It is the now where God has placed us, and it is the now where we need to worship Him.

Spend some time reflecting on the following:

1. Meditate on Psalm 46:10, "Be still, and know that I am God" (RSV). Spend the time in silence in the presence of Our Lord worshiping Him.

2. Meditate on Psalm 62:1, "For God alone my soul waits in silence; / from him comes my salvation" (RSV). Let your heart plead with God in silence for His grace.

3. Meditate on Ecclesiastes 3:7, which reminds us that there is a time for every purpose under heaven, "a time to keep silence, and a time to speak" (RSV). Ask God for the grace to know when you should be silent and when you need to speak.

Prayer

Lord, in the silence reveal yourself to me and teach me to know who you have created me to be and what I should do. Fill me with your love and drive out all fear that I may feel at this moment. Amen.

23
Meaning in Suffering

"Courage, daughter! Your faith has saved you."
— MATTHEW 9:22 (NAB)

Bishop Sheen

Pain in itself is not unbearable; it is the failure to understand its meaning that is unbearable. If that thief did not see purpose in pain he would never have saved his soul. Pain can be the death of our soul, or it can be its life.

It all depends on whether or not we link it up with Him Who, "having joy set before him, endured the cross." One of the greatest tragedies in the world is wasted pain. Pain without relation to the cross is like an unsigned check — without value. But once we have it countersigned with the Signature of the Saviour on the Cross, it takes on an infinite value.

A feverish brow that never throbs in unison with a Head crowned with thorns, or an aching hand never borne in patience with a Hand on the Cross, is sheer waste. The world is worse for that pain when it might have been so much the better.

All the sick-beds in the world, therefore, are either on the right side of the Cross or on the left; their position is determined by whether, like the thief on the left, they ask to be taken down, or, like the thief on the right, they ask to be taken up. It is not so much what people suffer that makes the world mysterious; it is rather how much they miss when they suffer. They seem to forget that even as children they made obstacles in their games in order to have something to overcome.

Why, then, when they grow into man's estate, should there not be prizes won by effort and struggle? Cannot the spirit of man rise with adversity as the bird rises against the resistance of the wind? Do not the game fish swim upstream? Must not the alabaster box be broken to fill the house with ointment? Must not the chisel cut away the marble to bring out the form? Must not the seed falling to the ground die before it can spring forth into life? Must not the little streams speed into the ocean to escape their stagnant self-content? Must not grapes be crushed that there may be wine to drink, and wheat ground that there may be bread to eat?

Why, then, cannot pain be made redemption? Why under the alchemy of Divine Love cannot crosses be turned into crucifixes? Why cannot chastisements be regarded as penances? Why cannot we use a cross to become God-like?

— From *The Rainbow of Sorrow*

Reflection

Bishop Sheen points out two ways to deal with life's burdens. One way crushes us, creating a feeling that there is no hope and that we have finally been defeated. Is not this way a hell on earth?

The other is to see the redemptive value of whatever burden it is that we may face. It is not something to blame on God (for indeed most pain comes to us from our own or someone else's folly), but rather something to turn to God as the only one who can liberate us.

As Bishop Sheen points out, we become like Christ in doing so. We should bring all of our pain and misfortune to the cross of Jesus and there reflect on what the value of our suffering is worth in eternity.

Sadly many today are ill equipped to deal with the pain, suffering, and misfortune that are part of every human life. Our culture seeks to remove all of these from our midst so that we fantasize that we can make a heaven of this earthly kingdom. But alas, heaven for one person often is hell for the rest.

Those who see the redemptive value of their suffering truly are Christlike. They make the people of our culture uncomfortable. But we should ask: How many crosses will we remove ourselves from, only to be nailed to new ones? When will we accept our crosses and follow in the footsteps of Our Lord?

+ + +

Spend some time reflecting on the following:

1. Meditate on Matthew 9:22, "Courage, daughter! Your faith has saved you" (NAB). Ask Our Lord to give you the faith that is capable of saving you, no matter what life may bring your way.

2. Reflect on your life. How have you dealt with adversity? Do you see it coming from God as

punishment, or do you see it as an opportunity to rely on God for His love and grace?

3. Ask Jesus to take all of your suffering and pains and use them for the good of those souls that you bring to Him in prayer.

Prayer

Lord, help me to imitate the thief who looked to you in his moment of great need and asked you to remember him in your kingdom.
May his words ever be on my lips. Amen.

24
Go-Go's — Come-Come's

"Come to me, all who labor and are heavy laden,
and I will give you rest."
— MATTHEW 11:28 (RSV)

✠

Bishop Sheen

The two extremes which one finds in the modern
world are the Go-Go group and the Come-Come
group. The Go-Go's are the new breed; the Come-
Come's are the old breed. The Go-Go's believe that
man has only a horizontal relationship with other
men; the Come-Come's that man has only a vertical
relationship with God. The Go-Go's know only one
side of the Commandment — namely, the love of
neighbor. The others know only the love of God but
not the love of neighbor. The Go-Go's would build a
secular city, because God is dead. The Come-Come's
would build only a city of God, because the world is
evil. The Go-Go's are flowing rivers with no beds;
the Come-Come's are all beds and no flowing waters
of life.

The first are all action and no contemplation; the
second all theory and no practice. The Go-Go's are
pendulums without clocks, and the Come-Come's
clocks without pendulums; the Go-Go's live for the
present, the Come-Come's for the past. The Go-Go

group insists that sociology be the new theology, that Christianity is humanism, that spirituality is pragmatism, and that if religion is not wholly in the world and for the world, it should perish. The Come-Come group refuse to budge from where they are. To them, change is decay, a protest is rebellion, and in their minds the greatest contribution one can bring to the world is by remaining in the sanctuary, keeping the status quo, and observing the minutiae of liturgical protocol.

The real leaders are those who avoid these extremes — or better, combine both, for both were united in the Life of Christ. Almost the first word of Our Lord's public Life was "come" (John 1:39, Mark 1:17, Matt. 4:18). The final word of His public Life was "go" into the world (John 20:21, Matt. 28:19, Acts 1:8). First one must come to Him to learn, to be inspired, to find the ultimate goal of life, to discover meaning, purposes, the significance of justice and liberty. Then go among the nations, go to accomplish, go to serve, to wash feet, to feed the hungry, to establish equality, to pick up wounded men like good Samaritans.

— From *Footprints in a Darkened Forest*

Reflection

Most of us can probably identify with one of the two groups that Bishop Sheen mentions in the above meditation; but as he points out, we must strive to imitate Our Lord, who valued both but made neither an absolute at the expense of the other. We must ever come into the presence of the Lord and be quick to go into the world and to bring Our Lord's presence to all we meet.

If we reflect on the reasons that we identify with either the Come-Come or the Go-Go group, we can learn a lot about ourselves, our fears, and those aspects of our personality that are still in need of the Lord's redemptive power.

Our Lord can heal us and we should see it as something that we are in need of healing, for the members of the one group think that God is not necessary (thereby they neglect prayer), whereas the members of the other group believe they are not necessary (wasting the power that God has given them in prayer). Both are temptations from the evil one, and the world is not a better place as long as each group thrives apart from the other.

We can be distracted by so many things in life that are not important when in fact only two are: first, that we love God with all our hearts, souls, and minds; and, second, that we love our neighbor as ourselves.

+ + +

Spend some time reflecting on the following:

1. Meditate on some aspect of the life of Our Lord. Reflect on what was important to Him. Ask for the grace to imitate Him in all that you do this day.
2. Meditate on the words of Our Lord found at the beginning of this mediation. See Our Lord inviting you to come to Him and to spend this time with

Him in communion. Bring to the Lord all that burdens your heart and soul.

3. Meditate on one of the passages that Bishop Sheen highlights where Our Lord told His disciples to "go." Visualize Our Lord speaking these words to you. What is Jesus asking you to do?

Prayer

Lord, bid me to come to you and allow that the time I spend in your presence will give me knowledge of what you wish me to do as I leave here and go out into the world at your command. Amen.

25
The Rosary

Bishop Sheen

The beautiful truth is that there is no repetition in, "I love you." Because there is a new moment of time, another point in space, the words do not mean the same as they did at another time or space. A mother says to her son: "You are a good boy." She may have said it ten thousand times before, but each time it means something different; the whole personality goes out to it anew, as a new historical circumstance summons forth a new outburst of affection. Love is never monotonous in the uniformity of its expression. The mind is infinitely variable in its language, but the heart is not. The heart of a man, in the face of the woman he loves, is too poor to translate the infinity of his affection into a different word. So the heart takes one expression, "I love you," and in saying it over and over again, it never repeats. It is the only real news in the universe. That is what we do when we say the Rosary, we are saying to God, the Trinity, to the Incarnate Saviour, to the Blessed Mother: "I love you, I love you, I love you." Each time it means something different because, at each decade, our mind is moving to a new demonstration of the Saviour's love: for example, from the mystery of His Love which willed to become one of us in His Incarnation, to the other mystery of love when He suffered for us, and on to the other mystery of His Love where He intercedes for us before the Heavenly Father. And who shall forget that Our Lord Himself in the moment of His greatest agony repeated, three times within an hour, the same prayer?

The beauty of the Rosary is that it is not merely a vocal prayer. It is also a mental prayer. One sometimes hears a dramatic presentation in which, while the human voice is speaking, there is a background of beautiful music, giving force and dignity to the words. The Rosary is like that. While the prayer is being said, the heart is not hearing music, but it is meditating on the Life of Christ all over again, applied to his own life and his own needs. As the wire holds the beads together, so meditation holds the prayers together. We often speak to people while our minds are thinking of something else. But in the Rosary we not only *say* prayers, we *think* them. Bethlehem, Galilee, Nazareth, Jerusalem, Golgotha; Calvary, Mount Olivet, Heaven — all these move before our mind's eye as our lips pray. The stained-glass windows in a church invite the eye to dwell on thoughts about God. The Rosary invites our fingers, our lips, and our heart in one vast symphony of prayer, and for that reason is the greatest prayer ever composed by man.

— From *The World's First Love*

Reflection

St. Luke tells us in his Gospel that Our Blessed Lady "treasured all these things in her heart" (Luke 2:51, *New International Version*), referring to the events of Our Lord's life. The Rosary is the prayer in which we imitate Mary and join her in meditating on Our Lord's divine plan. The repetition of the Hail Marys is a constant entreaty for her to join us as we join her in treasuring all that Our Lord accomplished in His life and finally also glorying with her over her Assumption and Crowning as Queen of Heaven.

Bishop Sheen in his meditation on the Rosary dwells on this repetition as something that is normal in the course of human events. We often repeat meaningful phrases that change meaning based on the events that correspond with them. Each time we pray the Rosary, our meditation is different because we are different. What we bring to prayer is not the same.

Our Lord, as Bishop Sheen points out, prayed the same prayer three times in the course of an hour while in His agony in the Garden of Gethsemane. The words were the same, but the experience was different each time He returned from finding those who were His companions asleep.

People often complain that they have difficulty meditating on the mysteries of the Rosary. They announce the mystery and begin the Our Father, then the Hail Marys, and quickly find that their mind is not on the mystery they have just announced but rather on an event that either has taken place that day or is yet to occur. This is not necessarily a distraction but rather may be the fruit of meditation. When you find yourself having such thoughts, reflect back on what the mystery is and ask yourself what the two have in common. You are apt to find a message that will bear much fruit in your life in that connection.

+ + +

Spend some time reflecting on the following:

1. Pray the Joyful Mysteries of the Rosary. Meditate on the mysteries, trying to vividly imagine each in detail. Ask the Lord for the graces that you need.

2. Pray the Sorrowful Mysteries of the Rosary. Meditate on the Passion of Our Lord and reflect on the suffering of His mother as she witnesses the death of her Son who dies for love of us. Ask for the grace to always have a heart that gives thanks to God.

3. Pray the Glorious Mysteries of the Rosary. Meditate on the joy the Mother of God must have felt upon seeing her Son alive again. Ask the Lord for the grace of a lively faith to believe in Him and for hope that you may share in His resurrection as His mother has in her Assumption into Heaven.

Prayer

Lord, help me never to tire of telling you how much I love you and need you. Teach me to give thanks at all times. Amen.

26
Our Father

Bishop Sheen

All men are one because God made man. Paul, a Jew, standing on the hill of the Areopagus, declared this great truth to the Senators of Greece: "God . . . hath made of one, all mankind, to dwell upon the whole face of the earth." And then, as if to remind them that this was not the teaching of his people alone, he quoted for them Aratus and Cleathus, saying: *"As some also of your poets said: For we are also his offspring."*

The world became united only in those periods of history when men recognized the overlordship of God. It was because the pagan, Cyrus, recognized that he was an instrument in the hands of God of Israel that he could bring himself to respect the rights of a conquered people and order rebuilt for them the Temple of Jerusalem. Alexander the Great is quoted by Plutarch as saying: "God is the common father of all men." No wonder then that he ordered that every city and every state should open its gates to the exiled opponents of the party and that his own officers should take brides from among the conquered people. And who shall forget Cicero's words that "the universe is to be regarded as a single commonwealth, since all are subject to the heavenly law and divine intelligence of Almighty God."

These dim aspirations of pre-Christian times were but feeble echoes of the Hebrew truth that God "shall be called the God of the whole earth." All of them were but dim foreshadowings of the day when the whole world would be enrolled, when the King of Kings and the Lord of Lords should be born — Creator of all men, Redeemer who made all men one because of all men. How much wiser the pre-Christian pagan than our post-Christian pagan! To unite men there must be something outside men, just as to tie up a bundle of sticks there must be someone outside the sticks. A moral law outside of nations to which all nations can appeal, and to which they must submit even when the decision goes against them, is the only condition of world peace. That is why we say there will never be one world until we all learn to pray, "Our Father, who art in Heaven."

— From *Seven Pillars of Peace*

Reflection

It may be lost on people now, but the modern civil rights movement was essentially fostered by Christian ministers who came to see the truth of what Bishop Sheen had said in 1944: The equality of people effectively rests on our acknowledging that there is one God and we are all His children.

Perhaps that is why most modern attempts to bolster equality fail. People have left God out of the picture. Whereas Christian ministers walked hand in hand in the marches from Selma to Montgomery and the brotherhood of all under one God was proclaimed, now no one dares mention the name of God.

In a sense God has taken the place of the marginalized in our modern world. It is God now who is segregated and not welcome in the public schools. It is God now who is left out in the public eating-places so that one seldom sees grace said before a meal. It is God who is no longer welcome on the sporting field. If humans need a scapegoat to place all of their sins upon and send out into exile, then surely God has taken on this role for Himself in our modern age.

But alas, without God, we fall back into familiar patterns of abuse of one another. Our Lord told a parable of a master who went on a trip and whose servants began abusing one another because they felt their master would not return. But eventually the master did return. God too will return when we least expect Him.

Equality is only possible if we believe that we all are children of one Father; that is why we say with Bishop Sheen, "Our Father, who art in heaven, hallowed be thy name. . . ."

+ + +

Spend some time reflecting on the following:

1. Say the Our Father very slowly. Pause now and then when something strikes you in the prayer and spend time reflecting on the meaning of the words.

2. Meditate on the words of John 17:20–21, quoted at the beginning of this section. Reflect on where unity is lacking in your life whether at home, at work, or in your neighborhood. What can you do to make a difference? Ask for the grace to do this.

3. Reflect on Our Lord's relationship with His Father and how He shares that relationship with us. Give thanks to the Father for His Son; give thanks to the Son for sharing His relationship with the Father with us. Ask for the grace to grow ever closer to the Trinity.

Prayer

Lord, help us to praise the Father in all that we do and to treat one another as brothers and sisters by following the example that you have set for us. Amen.

27
The New Creation

Therefore, if any one is in Christ, he is a new creation;
the old has passed away, behold, the new has come.
— 2 CORINTHIANS 5:17 (RSV)

Bishop Sheen

[Our Lord] placed the blame for chaos not on money but on men; not on politics but on politicians; not on military strategy but on generals; not on dictatorship but on dictators; not on money-lending but on the money-lenders. All these things had to be revolutionized, but the way to revolutionize them is first to revolutionize man. Therefore He said nothing about slavery, but He said everything about the dignity of a man; He said nothing about finances, but everything about the rich men who like Dives luxuriate their way to hell; He said nothing about violence against capitalism, but everything about violence against the selfishness of the man who lays up treasures which rust consumes and moths eat. He said nothing against armament, but He said everything against the man who draws his sword in hate. It was man who had to be reborn, to die to himself, to take up his daily cross, to cut off his hands of selfishness, to pluck out his eyes of envy, to become as a servant if he were a master, to bless if he were persecuted, to forgive if he were reviled, to rejoice if he were hated and above all else to die to his lower life, like a seed falling to the ground that he might live in the newness of a resurrected life where man lives even when the world dies. And so, He left Pilate in his judgment seat, Herod with his court, Annas with his Sanhedrin, soldiers on their streets, Caesar on his throne, and chose twelve men whom He remade in His Image and filled with His Spirit and sent them out to conquer the world and its institutions.

Naturally the world which placed its hope in the reformation of institutions could hardly tolerate the doctrine of Him Who placed the hope for reformation in a new man.

— From *Liberty, Equality and Fraternity*

Reflection

It could be that too much time is spent today pointing out what is wrong with the world and not enough time spent on what is wrong with us. As long as our focus is on the big picture, we can conveniently ignore the little one — ourselves.

Our relationship with Our Lord cannot help but change us and in the same way change the world around us. If we have the mind of Christ, then we will begin to see the world around us in a different way.

Those who practice praying in the presence of the Lord experience this. Her prayer before the Blessed Sacrament fueled the heroic virtue of Mother Teresa every morning.

We may fret about the world around us, but it is only in our power to allow Christ to change us. When we see with His eyes of love and mercy, then we will act in a way that will change those whom we come into contact with on a daily basis. If enough change takes place, the world will change.

Bishop Sheen's meditation recalls that we are not to be the same as we were before our contact with Our Lord. In the same way that the fishermen became fishers of men, we should not leave the presence of Our Lord with quite the same vocation that we came into His presence with.

+ + +

Spend some time reflecting on the following:

1. Meditate on Matthew 9:9, the Call of Matthew. Reflect on how Our Lord finds Matthew and how Matthew's life is changed in a moment when he encounters Jesus. How might this encounter with Jesus be changing you?

2. Reflect on 2 Corinthians 5:17 (quoted above). What does St. Paul mean when he says that anyone who is in Christ is a new creation? How does this bear fruit in your life?

3. Ask the Lord for the grace to change the world around you. Ask Him what He wishes you to do.

Prayer

Lord, change our minds to reflect your mind. Give us your attitude so that we see the world with your eyes. Fill us with your Holy Spirit so that we may be empowered to go out and fulfill the mission that you give us in this world. Amen.

28
When You Fail

There is no fear in love, but perfect love casts out fear. For fear has to do with punishment, and he who fears is not perfected in love.
— 1 JOHN 4:18 (RSV)

Bishop Sheen

When you fail to measure up to your Christian privilege, be not discouraged for discouragement is a form of pride. The reason you are sad is because you looked to yourself and not to God; to your failing, not to His Love: You will shake off your faults more readily when you love God than when you criticize yourselves. The sick person looks happily at the physician, not at his wounds. You have always the right to love Him in your heart, even though now and then you do not love Him in your acts. Keep no accounts with God or you will always be so hopelessly in debt as to be bankrupt.

Do not fear God for perfect love casteth out fear. God is biased in your favor. Would you rather be judged by the Justice of the Peace of your town on the last day, or by the King of Peace? Most certainly by God, would you not? David even chose a punishment at God's hands rather than man's for God he knew would be more lenient.

God is more lenient than you because He is perfectly good and, therefore, loves you more. Be bold enough, then, to believe that God is on your side, even when you forget to be on His. Live your life then, not by law, but by love. As St. Augustine put it: "Love God and then do whatever you please." If you love God, you will never do anything to hurt Him, and, therefore, never make yourself unhappy.

— From *Preface to Religion*

Reflection

Most of us may have grown up thinking of self-criticism as a form of spirituality. Certainly examining our conscience is a valid spiritual exercise, but focusing on our faults at the expense of God's love and mercy can, as Bishop Sheen says, be nothing less than a sinful exercise of our pride.

In Sacred Scripture the voice that we hear constantly telling us that we are not "all right" or not worthy to be in God's presence (which is true enough) is Satan. One of the meanings of the word Satan is "the accuser." In fact, that is how he is described in the Book of Zechariah where he stands on one side of Joshua the high priest, accusing him before God (see Zechariah 3).

In the Book of Revelation we read that one of the effects of Our Lord's triumph is that in the end the accuser (Satan) is cast out, and no longer will he be allowed to accuse us day and night before the Lord.

If we are to become like Our Lord, we must be like Him in focusing our lives on His love rather than on our faults. Our faults need to be confessed to a priest and then let go of in an act where we trust in the mercy and love of God to empower us to live in His love.

Bishop Sheen often preached about the way Satan appears to us before and after sin. Before, he appears as a friend (as he did to Eve in the Garden of Eden), telling us, "You have needs; certainly God doesn't expect you to forgo this." But after we commit a sin he appears as the accuser, smugly pointing out, "Now you've done it! You might as well go on sinning, since there is no hope for you!"

Most of us can relate to the message of Satan because we tend to listen to his voice rather than Our Lord's. Sacramental confession is the way to leave our sins where they belong — in the past. Our focus should always be on how much we need God's love and how with God's love we can be changed forever.

+ + +

Spend some time reflecting on the following:

1. Meditate on Matthew 14:22-33, the Gospel account of Jesus walking on the water. Notice that when Jesus bade Peter to come to him, Peter too walked on the water until he took his eyes off Jesus and took account of the wind. Reflect on how our sins are often tied into our taking our eyes off the Lord and concentrating on our environment instead.

2. Meditate on Zechariah. Notice how Satan works and how the angel of the Lord works. Reflect on what type of inner talk you conduct with yourself

on a daily basis. Do you listen to God's love or Satan's accusations?

3. Reflect on your failures. Ask God for the grace to see these as opportunities for His love and mercy to come into your life.

Prayer

Lord, when you fell on the road to Calvary three times, you rose three times. Give me the strength never to be crushed by my failures but rather to learn from you and your mercy. Amen.

29
The Anti-Christ

Be sober, be watchful. Your adversary the devil prowls around like a roaring lion, seeking some one to devour.
— 1 PETER 5:8 (RSV)

✠

Bishop Sheen

The anti-Christ will not be so called, otherwise he would have no followers. He will wear no red tights, nor vomit sulphur, nor carry a trident, nor wave an arrow tail as the Mephistophiles in Faust. This masquerade has helped the devil convince men that he does not exist, for he knows that he is never so strong as when men believe that he does not exist. When no man recognizes, the more power he exercises. God has defined Himself as "I am Who am" and the devil as "I am who am not."

Nowhere in Sacred Scripture do we find warrant for the popular myth of the devil as a buffoon who is dressed like the first "red." Rather is he described as an angel fallen from heaven, and as "the Prince of this world" whose business it is to tell us that there is no other world. His logic is simple: if there is no heaven there is no hell; if there is no hell, then there is no sin; if there is no sin, then there is no judge, and if there is no judgment then evil is good and good is evil.

But above all these descriptions, Our Lord tells us that he will be so much like Himself that he would deceive even the elect — and certainly no devil we have ever seen in picture books could deceive even the elect. How will he come in this new age to win followers to his religion? He will come disguised as the Great Humanitarian; he will talk peace, prosperity and plenty not as means to lead us to God, but as ends in themselves. He will write books on the new idea of God to suit the way people live; induce faith in astrology so as to make not the will but the stars responsible for sins; he will explain guilt away psychologically as inhibited eroticism, make men shrink in shame if their fellowmen say they are not broadminded and liberal; he will be so broadminded as to identify tolerance with indifference to right and wrong, truth and error; he will spread the lie that men will never be better until they make society better and thus have selfishness to provide fuel for the next revolution; he will foster science but only to have armament makers use one marvel of science to destroy another; he will foster more divorces under the disguise that another partner is "vital"; he will increase love for love and decrease love for person; he will invoke religion to destroy religion; he will speak of Christ and say that He was the greatest man who ever lived. . . .

He wants no proclamation of immutable principles from the lofty heights of a Church, but mass organization through propaganda where only a common man directs the idiosyncrasies of common men.

Opinions not truths, commentators not teachers, Gallup polls not principles, nature not grace — and to these golden calves will men toss themselves from their Christ.

— From Light Your Lamps

Reflection

I decided to include this passage from Bishop Sheen in this section on becoming more like Christ for several reasons. First, this selection was written by the bishop in 1950 but reads like a critique of the present day. Second, in order to become like Christ we must always be aware of the traps that the devil sets to keep us from fully embracing Christ. As the bishop points out, there is a thin line between Jesus Christ and the anti-Christ; but that thin line makes all the difference in the world — both this one and the one to come.

Our Lord counseled His disciples not to judge others and again we must be careful not to turn this meditation into a judgment of the people around us. But we should take a deep look at ourselves. When we think of Our Lord and the demands that a relationship with Him entails, do we focus on the truth that is revealed through Him in the Church or do we take account of the latest opinion poll?

As Bishop Sheen was fond of pointing out in his preaching, "God's ways are not our ways." Eighty-four percent of the Israelites thought it was unsafe to move into the promised land even after God had delivered them from the hands of the mighty Egyptians. For this they were forced to wander in the desert for another forty years (see Numbers 13:1—14:38).

When Our Lord announced that He was the Bread of Life in the sixth chapter of John's Gospel, many of His disciples no longer followed Him.

The truth is not an opinion poll. Peace is not something gained by the watering down of beliefs. Science and other disciplines can become very dangerous if a higher moral law no longer guides them.

We live on the verge of a great time of crisis. The words of Bishop Sheen are truer today than when he first penned them. We must ask ourselves, whose side are we on?

+ + +

Spend some time reflecting on the following:

1. Meditate on 2 Corinthians 11:14, which warns us that "even Satan disguises himself as an angel of light" (RSV). Reflect on what ways evil can be masked as a good in our society as well as in your own life. Ask God for the grace of discernment.

2. Reread Bishop Sheen's meditation. Reflect on current situations that seem to be "good" but in fact could be evil. How can you make a difference in these situations? Ask God for guidance and the courage to act to make the world more Christlike.

3. Reflect on the course of your entire life. Try to pick out the times that you have been led astray by evil. What appeared to be the good at the time? What in fact was the evil? Ask God for the grace to discern His Spirit in all of your choices.

Prayer

Lord, give us your light to see the way we should walk today and every day. Keep us from all evil. Give us the ability to discern when something is not of your will even when it presents itself to us as an angel of light. Amen.

30
Salve Regina

Bishop Sheen

I wish that each of us when we say the Rosary for
Peace would conclude it with the *Salve Regina* as
sung by the silent Trappists. Whenever I say that
prayer I recall the ten days I spent giving the Retreat to the Trappist monks in the Monastery of Our
Lady of Gethsemane, Kentucky. Nominally, I gave a
retreat to those 215 holy men, but really they gave a
retreat to me. As you know they lead lives of silence,
using speech only for prayer. At the close of the day
when their seven hours of formal prayer are ended,
all the lights are turned out in the Chapel. In this
total darkness they begin singing in Latin, the "Hail
Holy Queen, Mother of Mercy, our life, our sweetness and our hope." At that moment the large stained
glass window at the end of the long nave, which
one could not see in the darkness, begins to be illumined and shows a faint flickering of light. First one
sees the face of the Blessed Virgin, at which time

the voices of these holy men, as if inspired by the beauty of the Saviour's Mother, burst into song more vibrant, more heartfelt than any hymn of their day. The light now begins to suffuse more of the window, one can now see the Blessed Mother holding the Divine Child. His very presence intensifies their need of her intercession, as the Chapel echoes with the words: "To thee do we cry, poor banished children of Eve; to thee do we send forth our sighs, mourning and weeping in this valley of tears." By this time the whole window is illumined with the saints of the Trappist order, all gathered around Our Lady and her Divine Son. Feeling themselves one with that great family their exultant song goes on: "Turn then most Gracious Advocate, thine eyes of mercy towards us, and after this our exile show unto us the blessed fruit of thy womb, Jesus." No men in the world sing like the Trappists in their night song to Our Lord and His Lady. Here are over two hundred men all in love — and with the same Woman! And without jealousy, in wild tranquility, they ask but one favor: that she betray them with the "starry treachery of her eyes" into the Heart of Her Divine Son.

As John the Baptist leaped in the womb of His mother at the sight of the Blessed Virgin, so do these monks, locked in the dark *womb* of contemplation, leap like other Johns at the Virgin's Presence and as one of them put it: "Receive Christ into our night with stabs of intelligence as white as lightning."

— From *The Woman*

Reflection

A visitor to the Abbey of Gethsemane in Kentucky will encounter some changes following the many years that have passed since Bishop Sheen gave his retreat to the monks there. Today as one approaches the abbey church to the right, one sees the entrance to the cloister with the words "God Alone" engraved in the stone near the entrance.

The window that Bishop Sheen spoke of is no longer present within the abbey church. The church, which was renovated in the 1960s, is barren save the monks' choir. But the monks still end their night with the *Salve Regina* as they did when the bishop wrote of their love for Our Lady over half a century ago.

I remember the first time that I visited the chapel some twenty years ago, expecting to see the window ablaze as I attended Compline in the chapel. Of course, there was no window, but it did seem that the image of Our Lady holding the Divine Child was somehow engraved into the white brick in the nave of the building. It could have been my imagination, yet I could see it faintly but clearly.

The Blessed Mother is our mother also. In the same way that Our Lord permitted us to call God our Father, He also presented His mother to us from the cross, declaring her to be our mother. In her we are formed more perfectly into another Christ.

Devotion to her can only lead us more perfectly to Him. Love for her is a sign that we are truly part of the family in which God is our Father. She is the hope of all Christians because she is the first Christian. She was the first to say "yes" to Christ and the first to share in the fruits of His resurrection.

Like the monks at Gethsemane who, praying the prayer of the Church, end their nights singing her praises and asking her intercession, we too should cry out to her, begging her to pray "that we may be made worthy to share in the promises of Christ."

+ + +

Spend some time reflecting on the following:

1. Meditate on the words found on Gethsemane's cloister today, "God Alone." Ask God for the grace to always stay focused on Him as the Blessed Virgin was in her life.

2. Meditate on the Blessed Mother's care for the child Jesus. See in this care and concern a model for your prayer life. How well do you care for Jesus in your daily life? Is He your focus?

3. Pray the *Salve Regina* ("Hail Holy Queen"), slowly reflecting on the meaning of each word. Ask God for the grace to have a strong devotion to His Mother and yours.

Prayer

Hail, Holy Queen, Mother of Mercy, our life, our sweetness, and our hope! To thee do we cry, poor banished children of Eve. To thee do we send up our sighs, mourning and weeping in this valley of tears! Turn, then, O most gracious Advocate, thine eyes of mercy toward us, and after this, our exile, show unto us the blessed fruit of thy womb, Jesus. O clement, O loving, O sweet Virgin Mary.

Pray for us, O holy Mother of God, that we may be made worthy of the promises of Christ.

Appendix I

War and Peace

As mentioned in the Introduction, I decided to add this section after the events of September 11, 2001, when terrorists hijacked four commercial planes and changed forever our complacent attitude that we are safe from fanatics bent on toppling this great country.

Bishop Sheen penned the material in this appendix over sixty years ago; but like the other material in this book written by him, it is as relevant today as it was then and to whatever the future might hold. Someone familiar with the Church's teaching will come across the statement that "war is punishment from God for our sins." I think that the bishop's meditation on this puts it into context and helps us to understand exactly what that statement means.

The second meditation is on the power of God. The bishop focuses on the empty tomb as a sign of God's ultimate victory. It calls to mind the smoldering remains of ground zero where the World Trade Center once stood. Hopefully the reader will draw from this meditation that no matter how dark the present moment, the Christian's focus should always be on God, who has the power to rescue us from death and darkness.

31
War as a Judgment of God

Let the earth listen, and all that fills it;
the world, and all that comes from it.
For the LORD is enraged against all nations,
and furious against all their host,
he has doomed them, has given them over for slaughter.
— ISAIAH 34:1-2 (RSV)

Bishop Sheen

When I speak of war as a Judgment of God, I do not mean that it is a punishment in the sense of being an arbitrary action on the part of God, but in the sense of being an execution of the law of justice; men are visited with the effects of their own sins. In other words, sin brings adversity and such adversity is the expression of God's chastisement of sin, brought about by the action of man himself.

We are living in such a period of history now — the sad hour wherein we are gathering the bitter fruits of our apostasy from God. Wars from without; class hatreds, bigotry, anti-Semitism, anti-Catholicism, atheism, and immoralities from within — are the harvest of our godlessness. I know that there are many who profess belief in God, but they do not act on that belief. What recognition is given to the moral law in politics, economics, or education? How many Americans who say they believe in God went to their church or synagogue today to give thanks to Him? Do we forget that the evil fruits which St. Paul in the first century told the Romans would ripen on the tree of godlessness are now ripening on the tree of America's godlessness? . . . Then if we turn to St. James we learn that not only is our national crime due to godlessness but even wars as well, "From whence are wars and contentions among you? Are they not hence, from your concupiscences, which war in your members?" (James 4:1)

We shall do either one of two things: Recognize the fact of God's judgment or have it proved against us. If we acknowledge it, and act accordingly, then it shall be made good in us by repentance, restoration and peace, as it was in the soul of the Good Thief who recognized the just deserts of his sins; and we shall cry out in the language of the Scripture: "We have sinned, do thou unto us whatsoever pleaseth thee: only deliver us this time" (Judges 10:15).

Or, if we resist the Judgment of God, it shall be proved against us nevertheless by His Power as it was against the city of Jerusalem, which knew not the time of its visitation. Our greatness is conditioned upon our earnestness in examining our own faults and remedying them. . . .

The choice is clear: We will as a nation either go back to God and the moral law and faith in Christ, or we will corrupt from within. In exiling God from our national life, our politics, our economics, and our education, it was not His Heart we pierced — it was America we slew! May God forgive us!

— From *War and Guilt*

Reflection

Our Lord was sinless, yet He suffered a horrible death on the cross. We know from revelation that it was our sins that put Him on that cross. How many other innocents suffer for our sins?

What has the unborn done to either mother or father who consents to the abortion? Is it not their sin for which the innocent suffers?

What have the children of any nation done to suffer the ravages of war? Is it not the sins of the adults that bring upon them the devastation that they suffer?

Bishop Sheen gives us a choice and points us in the direction of the good thief, who realizes that he is not innocent and that the punishment that he is receiving he deserves. We should likewise not fool ourselves in thinking that the multitude of our sins have not caused the suffering of others. We should cry out in faith like the good thief and repent.

To repent means to "turn around," to face in a different direction. Often it is the practice for Christians and Jews to physically face the east and for Muslims to face Mecca when praying. It is a physical act connoting a more spiritual one, namely that of turning away from whatever holds my attention at the moment and turning my attention to God.

We tend to act as though something is always more important than God. This in itself is sin. For if we truly believe that God is who God is, there is nothing more important. As Jean Pierre de Caussade says, "Without God everything is nothing, with God nothing is everything."

+ + +

Take some time to reflect on the following:

1. How have your sins contributed to the suffering of others? Ask God to forgive you for your sins and to ease the suffering that you have caused others.

2. How have the sins of our nation caused others to suffer? Pray for the leaders of your local, state, and federal government that God will give them good judgment in all their actions that they may act with the welfare of all in mind.

3. Pray for an end to all war.

Prayer

Lord Jesus, we deserve to suffer for our sins. Please forgive us and our nation for all that we have done to hurt others. Heal our wounds and give us the grace to turn to you again. Amen.

32
The Power of God

See the place where they laid him.
— MARK 16:6 (RSV)

☩

Bishop Sheen

There emerges the Easter lesson that the power of evil and chaos of any one moment can be defied and conquered, for the basis of our hope is not the construct of human power, but in the Power of God Who has given to the evil of this earth its one mortal wound — an empty tomb, a gaping sepulchre, an empty grave.

Apply the Easter lesson to the Dark Hour in which we now live. Whence shall come our hope of victory? Shall it be in the power of arms alone? Shall it be in the power of the common man alone?

Our hope for victory in this war must not be in the power of arms alone, for the enemy has the Devil on his side, and guns, planes, tanks, and shells are no match for Boasts.

As Isaias warned: "Woe to them that go down to Egypt for help, trusting in horses, and putting their confidence in chariots, because they are many: and in horsemen, because they are very strong; and have not trusted in the Holy One of Israel, and have not sought after the Lord." (Isa. 31:1-2)

Let the enemy come as so many armored and panoplied Goliaths thinking that steel must always be met by steel alone, and we shall, like other Davids, go out to meet them unto victory clothed in the Power of Him Who gave to the evil of this earth its one mortal wound — an empty tomb, a gaping sepulchre, an empty grave.

Nor, on the other hand, should our hope for a more democratic way of life in the world be in the common man unpurified by faith; for once in power, he will cease to be the uncommon man purified by faith; for once in power, he will cease to be the common man of the proletariat and will become the uncommon man or the bureaucrat. The common man who trusts in flesh alone can be counted to abuse his power just as much as the class he overthrew.

Rather we must trust in the common man made uncommon by the Power of Him Who dared to say to the first of all Totalitarian Caesars of Christian History: "Thou shouldst not have any power . . . unless it were given thee from above." (John 19:11)

— From *The Divine Verdict*

Reflection

No matter how dark the present hour may seem for the Christian, there is always hope, even when the darkest moment is brought on by the death of a loved one. The empty tomb is the ultimate sign of God's power over the ultimate enemy of every human being — death.

The power of God manifest in the resurrection of Jesus is our constant hope. It enables us to "walk through the valley of death" with no fear, because God is at our side. Spending time in the presence of Our Risen Lord should give us that assurance.

Whatever may threaten us in this life, if God is for us, who can be against us? God is more powerful than anything that can come against us. As Jesus said, "Do not fear those who kill the body but cannot kill the soul; rather fear him who can destroy both soul and body in hell" (Matthew 10:28, RSV). Only God has the power to destroy both soul and body, and only a few verses later Jesus tells us, "Fear not, therefore; you are of more value than many sparrows" (Matthew 10:31, RSV). God loves us and desires us to be in communion with Him.

+ + +

Spend some time reflecting on the following:

1. Meditate on the resurrection of Our Lord. Think about the reality of the crucifixion, His death, and the expectation of the women and disciples who approached His tomb on Easter Sunday. Ask for the grace to believe with a strong faith in the power of God.

2. Tell Our Lord all that fills you with anxiety and fear. Ask for the grace of God's peace to fill your heart.

3. Reflect on the state of the world without God. Ask God to intervene in those areas of the world that seem most in need of His presence at this moment.

Prayer

Lord, give us the strength to trust in you with a lively faith that drives out all fear. Bring all to believe in you. Have mercy on us, O Lord!

Appendix II

✠

Prayers

$\mathcal{T}$he prayers in this section appear through the courtesy of Father Andrew Apostoli, C.F.R., who composed them. They are not "official" prayers and should only be prayed privately. These prayers are being used by those seeking special graces through the intercession of Bishop Sheen and for those who are praying for his canonization.

In December of 1999, on the twentieth anniversary of the death of Archbishop Sheen, Cardinal O'Connor of New York authorized the private investigation into the life of Archbishop Sheen by the Archbishop Fulton John Sheen Foundation. If you would like to share any personal knowledge of the archbishop (letters, photos, life experiences) or to report any spiritual or physical favors granted in his name, please send this information to Father Andrew at:

> Father Andrew Apostoli, C.F.R.
> St. Leopold Friary
> 59 Nepperhan Avenue
> Yonkers, NY 10701

Prayer to Obtain a Favor Through the Intercession of Archbishop Sheen

(For Private Use Only)

Eternal Father, You alone grant us every blessing in Heaven and on earth, through the redemptive mission of Your Divine Son, Jesus Christ, by the working of the Holy Spirit. In every age, You raise up men and women outstanding in holiness, whose faithful service has contributed significantly to the mission of the Church. In this very way, You used the life and work of Your servant, Archbishop Fulton John Sheen. He inspired great numbers of Catholics and other people of good will to grow in virtue and lead lives pleasing to You and of service to their brothers and sisters in need. He encouraged them to embrace the "Gospel of Life" by recognizing that in all its circumstances, "Life is worth living."

If it be according to Your Will, Eternal Father, glorify Your servant, Archbishop Fulton John Sheen, by granting the favor I now request through his prayerful intercession *(mention your request here)*. I make this prayer confidently in Jesus' Name, through the merits of His Passion, Death and Resurrection. Amen.

Prayer to Move the Church to Proclaim Archbishop Sheen a Saint

(For Private Use Only)

Heavenly Father, source of all good and all holiness, You reward those who love and serve You faithfully as Your sons and daughters. If it pleases You, I ask You to glorify Your servant, Archbishop Fulton John Sheen. He touched countless lives by his ministry of evangelization, especially through the media. His clear and courageous teachings about Jesus and the truths of the Catholic Church seemed to possess a special power of the Holy Spirit that strengthened the faithful and inspired many converts to embrace the Faith. He supported the needs of missionaries all over the world through his work in the National Office for the Propagation of the Faith. He also labored zealously for the renewal of the Priesthood by preaching retreats to his brother priests and by encouraging them with the good example of his daily Eucharistic Holy Hour. His deep personal love of Our Lady moved many others to go to Jesus through His mother.

Heavenly Father, if it be according to Your Divine Will, I ask You to move Your Church to glorify Your faithful servant, Archbishop Fulton John Sheen. I ask this prayer confidently in Jesus' Name. Amen.

Sources

+

(All by Fulton J. Sheen)

Calvary and the Mass, Garden City Books, Garden City, N.Y., 1953.

Footprints in a Darkened Forest, Meredith Press, New York, 1967.

Freedom Under God, The Bruce Publishing Co., Milwaukee, Wisc., 1940.

Fulton J. Sheen's Guide to Contentment, Simon and Schuster, New York, 1967.

Go to Heaven, A Chapel Book, Dell Publishing Co., Inc., New York, 1961.

Liberty, Equality and Fraternity, The Macmillan Co., New York, 1938.

Life Is Worth Living, Image Books, Garden City, N.Y., 1978.

Lift Up Your Heart, McGraw-Hill Book Co., Inc., New York, 1950.

Light Your Lamps, Our Sunday Visitor, Inc., Huntington, Ind., 1950.

Love One Another, Garden City Books, Garden City, N.Y., 1953.

Moods and Truths, The Century Co., New York and London, 1932.

Old Errors and New Labels, D. Appleton-Century Co., New York and London, 1937.

Peace of Soul, Permabooks, New York, 1954.

Preface to Religion, P. J. Kenedy and Sons, New York, 1946.

Seven Pillars of Peace, Charles Scribner's Sons, New York, 1944.

Seven Words to the Cross, P. J. Kenedy and Sons, New York, 1944.

The Cross and the Crisis, The Bruce Publishing Co., Milwaukee, Wisc., 1938.

The Divine Verdict, P. J. Kenedy and Sons, New York, 1943.

The Eternal Galilean, Garden City Publishing Co., Garden City, N.Y., 1934.

The Moral Universe, The Bruce Publishing Co., Milwaukee, Wisc., 1936.

The Mystical Body of Christ, Sheed and Ward, New York, 1935.

The Priest Is Not His Own, McGraw-Hill Book Co., Inc., New York, 1963.

The Rainbow of Sorrow, Garden City Books, Garden City, N.Y., 1938.

These Are the Sacraments, Hawthorne Books, Inc., New York, 1962.

The Seven Virtues, P. J. Kenedy and Sons, New York, 1940.

The Way of the Cross, Our Sunday Visitor, Inc., Huntington, Ind., 1982.

The Woman, Our Sunday Visitor, Inc., Huntington, Ind., 1952.

The World's First Love, Image Books, Doubleday and Co., Inc., Garden City, N.Y., 1954.

Those Mysterious Priests, Doubleday and Co., Inc., Garden City, N.Y., 1974.

Three to Get Married, Appleton-Century-Crofts, Inc., New York, 1951.

War and Guilt, Our Sunday Visitor, Inc., Huntington, Ind., 1941.

PRAYING IN THE PRESENCE OF
OUR LORD

PRAYERS FOR
EUCHARISTIC
ADORATION

FR. BENEDICT J. GROESCHEL, C.F.R.

A selection of prayers from the time
of the Fathers right up to our own day.
0-87973-586-4 (586), paper, 90 pp.

To order from Our Sunday Visitor:
Toll free: 1-800-348-2440
E-mail: osvbooks@osv.com
Website: www.osv.com

Availability of products subject to change without notice.

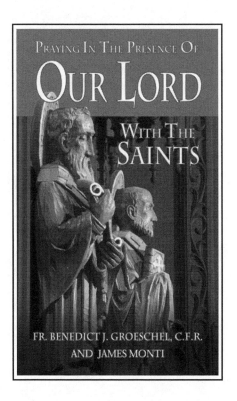

PRAYING IN THE PRESENCE OF

OUR LORD

WITH THE
SAINTS

FR. BENEDICT J. GROESCHEL, C.F.R.
AND JAMES MONTI

The very words used by the saints
of the Church in their own prayers.
0-87973-948-7 (948), paper, 112 pp.

To order from Our Sunday Visitor:
Toll free: 1-800-348-2440
E-mail: osvbooks@osv.com
Website: www.osv.com

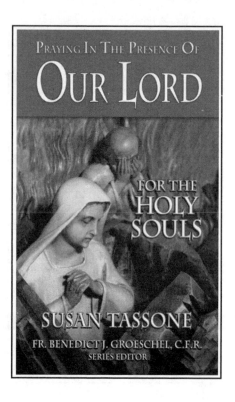

Perhaps the finest collection of prayers
for the souls in purgatory ever assembled.
0-87973-921-5 (921), paper, 144 pp.

To order from *Our Sunday Visitor*:
Toll free: 1-800-348-2440
E-mail: osvbooks@osv.com
Website: www.osv.com

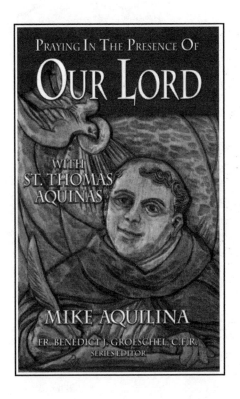

PRAYING IN THE PRESENCE OF

OUR LORD

WITH
ST. THOMAS
AQUINAS

MIKE AQUILINA

FR. BENEDICT J. GROESCHEL, C.F.R.
SERIES EDITOR

These poem-prayers will lift you up
to the pinnacle of Christian thought.
0-87973-958-4 (958), paper, 144 pp.

Our Sunday Visitor. . .
Your Source for Discovering
the Riches of the Catholic Faith

Our Sunday Visitor has an extensive line of materials for young children, teens, and adults. Our books, Bibles, booklets, CD-ROMs, audios, and videos are available in bookstores worldwide.

To receive a FREE full-line catalog or for more information, call **Our Sunday Visitor** at **1-800-348-2440**. Or write, **Our Sunday Visitor /** 200 Noll Plaza / Huntington, IN 46750.

- -

Please send me: ___A catalog

Please send me materials on:

___Apologetics and catechetics   ___Reference works

___Prayer books   ___Heritage and the saints

___The family   ___The parish

Name_____

Address_____Apt._____

City_____State_____Zip_____

Telephone (   ) _____

A23BBABP

- -

Please send a friend: ___A catalog

Please send a friend materials on:

___Apologetics and catechetics   ___Reference works

___Prayer books   ___Heritage and the saints

___The family   ___The parish

Name_____

Address_____Apt._____

City_____State_____Zip_____

Telephone (   ) _____

A23BBABP

- -

Our Sunday Visitor
200 Noll Plaza
Huntington, IN 46750
Toll free: 1-800-348-2440
E-mail: osvbooks@osv.com
Website: www.osv.com